Praise for *Where's Your Wow?*

"A sure-fire business classic! This book will catapult your career."
—Jack O'Dwyer, editor of
Jack O'Dwyer's newsletter

"Only the best brands are selling today. *Where's Your Wow?* shows you how to stand out in the clamoring crowd seeking fortune and fulfillment."
—Dr. Denis Waitley, author, *The Seeds of Greatness*

"If you want to be irresistible, successful, and extraordinary, read this book."
—Ken D. Foster, author of *Ask and You Will Succeed*
and CEO of Shared Vision Network

"Regardless of what business you're in, this incredible book will show you exactly how to stand out from the crowd, become magnetic, and smoke your competition!
—Larry Pinci and Phil Glosserman, coauthors of *Sell the Feeling:
The 6-Step System that Drives People to Do Business with You*

"Absolutely incredible! Clear, comprehensive, and loaded with fabulous stories!"
—David Hancock, CEO Morgan James Publishing

"I wish I had *Where's Your Wow?* back when I first started! This new book will help you to reach—and *monetize*—your personal brand potential. And that's *The Savage Truth*!"
—Terry Savage, author of T*he Savage Truth on Money*
and *The Savage Number*, syndicated *Chicago Sun-Times* columnist

"This is a *Wow* book that will have a *Wow* impact on your success!"
—Willie Jolley, award-winning speaker, best-selling author,
and syndicated radio show host

"I love *Where's Your Wow?*! Robyn and Rick have written an inspiring and meaningful book that is guaranteed to energize you personally and professionally."
—Barbara DeAngelis, Ph.D., No. 1 *New York Times* best-selling author and transformation teacher, *How Did I Get Here? Finding Your Way to Renewed Hope and Happiness When Life and Love Take Unexpected Turns*

"Your *Wow* awaits you within the pages of this wonderfully readable book. Read it, apply it, and go *Wow* the world!"
—Jay Conrad Levinson, the "father of guerrilla marketing," author, *Guerrilla Marketing* series of books

"When was the last time a product or service made you say *'Wow!'*? This wonder of a book will show you how to create that same magic in your own business."
—Ken Blanchard, coauthor of *The One Minute Manager* and *The One Minute Entrepreneur*

"If you're tired of living a mundane life, falling short of success, then you've come to the right book. Robyn and Rick brilliantly deliver the cure!"
—Les Brown, world-renowned motivational speaker

"Robyn and Rick are two of the best thinkers on this subject in the country. This book will give you tactics and strategies to create world-class results."
—Steve Gardner, partner Five Star Speakers and Trainers

"This powerful, practical book shows you how to position yourself and your business for more sales, faster and easier, in competitive markets."
—Brian Tracy, chairman and CEO of Brian Tracy International and best-selling author of *Speak to Win*

Where's Your WOW?

16

WAYS
**TO MAKE YOUR COMPETITORS
WISH THEY WERE _YOU_!**

Where's Your WOW?

16 WAYS

TO MAKE YOUR COMPETITORS WISH THEY WERE *YOU!*

•

Robyn Freedman Spizman and Rick Frishman

New York   Chicago   San Francisco   Lisbon   London
Madrid   Mexico City   Milan   New Delhi   San Juan   Seoul
Singapore   Sydney   Toronto

The McGraw·Hill Companies

1 2 3 4 5 6 7 8 9 0   DOC/DOC   0 9 8

ISBN 978-0-07-154519-8
MHID   0-07-154519-0

McGraw-Hill books are available at special quantity discounts to use as premiums and sales promotions, or for use in corporate training programs. To contact a representative please visit the Contact Us pages at www.mhprofessional.com.

This book is printed on acid-free paper.

Photo credit (Robyn): Keiko Guest Photography

Library of Congress Cataloging-in-Publication Data

Spizman, Robyn Freedman.
    Where's your wow? : sixteen laws for building your brand, catapulting your career, and standing out in the crowd / by Robyn Freedman Spizman and Rick Frishman.
        p. cm.
    Includes bibliographical references and index.
    ISBN 978-0-07-154519-8 (alk. paper)
    1. Career development. 2. Success in business. 3. Success. I. Frishman, Rick, 1954–
II. Title.
    HF5381.S7354   2008
    650.1–dc22   2008008355

To you—our reader. We hope that this little book
will inspire you in an extraordinary way.
May you discover your *Wow* and then put it to work!

c o n t e n t s

a c k n o w l e d g m e n t s

We are deeply thankful to the large number of talented, insightful, and generous individuals who helped us create this book. It began with the law offices of Lloyd J. Jassin, our agent/attorney, who spearheaded our efforts. Not only did Lloyd write the book on copyright law, but he is also a leading literary expert, and we are deeply indebted to him for his outstanding efforts on our behalf. We were equally fortunate when we met with Herb Schaffner at McGraw-Hill, who strategically went to bat for us with the vision that ultimately became this book. When you get assigned an editor as skillful and insightful as Herb Schaffner, you know you hit the lottery. That was clearly our lucky day! We also wish to thank the amazing McGraw-Hill team including: Philip Ruppel, president of MGH Professional, along with Ed Chupak, Seth Morris, Lydia Rinaldi, Kenya Henderson, and Daina Penikas. And our thanks go to Jack Heffron, who helped us tie this effort together with his brilliant ability to research and share stories that contributed to the success of this book. Jack, you *Wow*ed us right down to the wire, and we are forever grateful for your friendship and unwavering support.

In the tried and true tradition of taking our own advice, we teamed up with smarter people who we wish to thank. These talented and brilliant individuals either participated and loaned us their wisdom or assisted us in securing meaningful contacts to interview as we wrote this book. We wish to express our deepest thanks to

Wally Amos

Joel Babbit

Margo Berman

Ken Blanchard

Bruce Blythe

H. Jackson Brown

Jill Connor Browne

Stephen Burgay

Pat Burns

Jack Canfield

Alex Carroll

Patti Coffey

David D'Alessandro

Bryan and Jeffery Eisenberg

Deborah Fine

Jeanne Fitzmaurice

Edie Fraser

Doug and Genie Freedman

Becky Frusher

Five Star Speakers–Steve
    Gardner and Nicole
    Wienholt

Drs. Stephen and Marianne
    Garber

Sam Garrett

Randy Gilbert

Cynthia Good

Seth Goldberg

Stedman Graham

Doug Hall

David Hancock

Mark Victor Hansen

Steve Harrison

Paul Hartunian

Dennis Haskins

Judge Glenda Hatchett

Dan Heath

Gary and Diane Heavin

Dr. Henry Heimlich

Paul Hoffman

Michael Hutchinson

Tory Johnson

Willie Jolley

Michele Kapustka

Richard Kiel

Brian Kurtz

Joanne LaMarca Mathisen

Kenneth Jay Lane

Steve Lillo

Marissa Mayer

Joe Mark

Ken McArthur

Joseph Michelli

David Morrell

Jack Morton

Heidi Nel

Susan Packard

Karen Quinn

Laura Ries

William Ruder

David Sack

Mark Sanborn

Tim Sanders

Stuart and Shelby Stout

Roger Sweet

Joe Sugarman

Helen Taffet,
    sensationalbaskets.com

Linda Kaplan Thaler

Susan Tucker

Ari Weinzweig

Scott Wine

Sandra and Kym Yancey

Mel Zuckerman

From Robyn:

My life is filled with so many individuals who serve as the best gifts a girl could ever receive. Thanks to my outstanding coauthor, Rick Frishman: Working with you is such a privilege, and you never cease to amaze me! Thanks to my devoted family and true-life treasures who *Wow* me daily starting with my remarkable parents, Phyllis and Jack Freedman, my wonderful husband, Willy, and our greatest accomplishments in life, our children, Justin and Ali. You make it all worthwhile and cheer me on. Thanks to Doug and Genie Freedman and Sam and Gena Spizman for your love and support, along with The Spizman Agency, Jenny Corsey, Hayley Roberts, and my guardian angel, Bettye Storne, who knows what I want before I even ask! And thanks to my special aunts, Lois Blonder and Ramona Freedman, along with my entire extended family. I am fortunate to have you all in my life and hope that you know how much you mean to me. In addition, it also doesn't get any better than my outstanding circle of friends, too wonderful to attempt to describe without writing a lengthy book. You are the best life has to offer. I'm humbled by your friendship and love.

From Rick:

The first thank you goes to my wonderful coauthor, Robyn Spizman, who I have known for over 20 years and is one of the finest coauthors a guy could ask for. I wish to acknowledge Mike (Manny) Levine, who founded Planned Television Arts in 1962 and was my mentor and partner for over 18 years. Mike taught me that work has to be fun and meaningful and then the profits will follow. Thanks to my exceptional management team at PTA, you are the best in the business. Thanks also to Joy Smith for your wonderful support. And to my new family at Morgan James Publishing, it is an honor to be part of the team. David Hanlock you are the nicest man in publishing, and you are a true friend. And thanks to my brother Scott, who has always been there to support me in whatever I do. Thanks also to my children, Adam, Rachel, and Stephanie. Watching you grow into fine young individuals has been the highlight of my life. And to my wife, Robbi, you are my strength.

introduction

Wow!

We don't know of another word that casts the net so wide and captures the world of business so succinctly and successfully. *Wow* happens when you and your business, ideas, and abilities stand out in that very small zone called *distinctive*. You do something or handle yourself in a way that's so fresh, innovative, and impressive that you are memorable. And you make it look effortless.

We all search for *Wows* every day of our lives. Adding a *Wow* to your everyday world is adding a signature style that reflects who you are. It's not about outdoing someone else; it's about adding a spark in life that simply leaves a memorable mark. *Wow* keeps us alive and alert and inventing new and improved ways to do routine things. It keeps us doing really great work and being the best we can be at what we do. This sounds so cliché, but it's true. Be great at what you do. Find the little flame that lights a fire of *Wow* around your world and sets it ablaze.

And did we mention your attitude? We've all met *Wow* people. Everyone wants to be around them. They attract customers, supporters, readers, and purchasers, and they can help spread the word. They knock us off our feet with their energy and charisma, their confidence, or their style. From the boardroom to the mailroom, the classroom to the courtroom, the ball ground to the playground, no matter what they do, they bring a *Wow* to their work. They take nothing for granted and do little things in extraordinary ways.

What *Wow*-achievers and companies with a *Wow* have is a personal brand—an identity that others recognize. Whether it's for yourself or for a product or service you sell or for your business, you need to be extraordinary to be seen and heard amid the tumult of the marketplace. You need to find your *Wow* and then use it to push yourself into the spotlight. Remember: Ordinary is not extraordinary. The difference is *extra*.

Too often people find themselves doing what it takes just to get by. They become simply cogs in a great big wheel. With this type of mentality, it's tough to think creatively and to do what's necessary to rise to the top and stand out from the crowd. They lose a sense of what makes them special and what skills, ideas, and background they possess. They find themselves feeling frustrated, languishing in a business or job that's not giving them the success they want.

Does this description sound familiar? If so, you've arrived at the right place. Discovering that extra something about yourself and your work is key. And by chance if you're one of the *Wow* individuals we celebrate in this book and wish to honor, we sing your praises and stand in *Wow* and awe of you!

To discover your *Wow*, you first must be able to identify it—not just in terms of delivering a great product, idea, or service but on many levels that will catapult your success. In *Where's Your Wow?* you'll find a step-by-step guide to recognizing what makes you unique—your signature style—and learn how to systematically build your brand to heights that you would not have imagined possible. We're not saying that it's easy. We're not offering some facile "magic formula." We're offering wisdom based on our own experience and the experience of many other people who have achieved *Wow* success. We've distilled the essence of that wisdom and experience into 16 ways that, when followed, will bring you the success you dream about now.

Wow is the quality that sets you apart, that goes beyond the norm and delivers more than what's expected. It's a difference between you and the competition that is so dramatic that it grabs immediate attention. We've structured the book to help you achieve a *Wow* every step along the way to success—from envisioning that success through developing the idea to staying hungry after you've begun seeing results. *Wows* rarely happen overnight. They are built, one layer at a time, by following the guidelines we've put together in this book. The layers then blend to create new possibilities and more successes. We've pursued layers of the best stories and examples that will illustrate how to achieve

Wow in your work. We've uncovered stories that demonstrate how *Wow* rises to the top of mind. And as you read this book, remember that the whole of anything done well becomes stronger than any one layer on its own. Such is a fine-tuned marketing plan. It is just like a prize-winning layer cake made up of platforms of cake with irresistible icing, or an ice cream sundae layered with chocolate fudge and caramel and topped with nuts and a cherry, or a steaming hot tray of mouth-watering lasagna, where the layers and the flavors of its success meld together and become more successful when the parts of the whole work in tandem—one layer and one ingredient at a time merging its richness. The layers of *Wow*, like the layers of anything done well, create an overall experience that says *Wow*!

✳ FINDING YOUR WOW

We wrote this book with every reader in mind. Whether you come from a corporate culture or a field of academia, whether you are an entrepreneur or small-business owner, you hold the key to your personal and professional success. Discovering your *Wow* and what *Wows* others to help you fast-forward success will open the door to a more memorable and meaningful impact. Our experience and insights come from our over 50 collective years helping turn companies into the company you keep, expertise into experts, and authors into authorities. We went to the experts we admire most and layered the wisdom we felt you needed to know to break through the noisy messages that clutter the world today. And to all of them we are grateful for their affirmations and individual research. *Wow* is within all of us. It's not mystical. It's not expensive. It's about the rules of doing business, understanding yourself, and presenting yourself that have proven successful for many of the people we admire and read about. Success isn't an esoteric system; it's a matter of finding the qualities inside you that match a need in the marketplace and developing that match by following the elements of a sound business plan.

Every *Wow* is unique in itself, and every *Wow* shares common traits. This is why we have talked to so many people from so many fields to give you a broader and richer view of how success works than you'll find elsewhere. We've skimmed the cream from the top of dozens of fields to find out how they got there and to show you how you can get there too.

So who are we? Meet Robyn—think bionic. She's a prolific author, nationally recognized media personality, an idea-a-minute "think tank," and one of the country's foremost gift experts. Her entire platform is built on products and information that screams *Wow*! Meet Rick—one of the best-loved promoters and publicists in the country. He has represented some of the biggest companies, names, and experts in the business and is founder of Planned Television Arts. After we teamed up to write a definitive series on getting published, called *Author 101*, we decided that we had something simple but sensational to say that would help everyone get noticed. What good is your great idea, important service, or fabulous company if you can't get the ink, eyeballs, and ears you really deserve?

But first we agreed that the world didn't need one more same-old business book about success. However, we were confident that we held a different perspective of success that would help anyone and everyone from the largest companies in the world to the solo entrepreneur break into business arenas, even if they didn't have a breakthrough idea. With our combined experience, appearances on leading talk shows, dozens of books published, and helping unknown names become household names, we learned one great big thing along the way: If you understand your *Wow* and then make it happen in a *Wow* way with a *Wow* plan and a *Wow* platform, you are going to *Wow* 'em!

In fact, we contend that no matter who you are or what you do in life, to succeed, you will need to understand the true meaning of your own individual *Wow*—now. Although the concept of *Wow* seems fairly simple, once you see how others have leveraged their distinctiveness and left their mark in time, you'll be motivated to reach for even greater success. With the proper layering of your personal uniqueness, the possibilities for your success are endless.

You picked up this book because you want to be a tremendous success in life—both professionally and personally. And we are committed to helping you achieve that goal. We wrote this book to help you define, communicate, promote, market, and build your brand with an irresistible and identifiable edge. In simpler terms, we want to help you to claim your *Wow*!

☀ GET STARTED!

You needn't be a marketing expert to apply the laws of *Wow*. If you're a seasoned pro already, use this system to ensure that your plan has all the essential ingredients. When doing anything in business, you'll make sure that all the pieces are working together and piled high for success. Success is built on layers of experience, wisdom, and talent, but regardless of your experience, everyone can do it. Give it a try! With any great idea, when you don't take a risk, you may never know if you could have succeeded. So have no regrets and take a chance. Don't postpone that brilliant idea or business concept that you want to bring to life. With the right focus, determination, and insights into what makes you distinctive, you have a chance to play to your strengths, sharpen your edge, and catapult your success. Build the plan, and turn on the heat!

When you understand this premise, you'll move forward, creating one layer at a time. You'll discover that success is a process and that the joy that you bring to each layer makes the adventure worthwhile. Each friendship, acquaintance, opportunity, and accomplishment forms a reflection of the world you want to create. And the more lessons you learn and experiences you try, the greater are the rewards to help you accomplish a life well lived and well fed with inspiration.

Here's to your success—your *Wow* success!

PART **1**

What Makes You Special?

CHAPTER 1

Envision Your Success

The greatest danger for most of us is not that our aim is too high and we miss it, but that our aim is too low and we reach it.

—Unknown

It can start with little more than an inkling–a vague idea for a product, service, or brand or maybe just a sense of some new career path that you want to follow that offers more possibilities than the one you're on now. Although sometimes an idea hits us like a lightning bolt, in most cases it drifts more quietly into our minds–a tiny seed blown by the winds of inspiration.

Think for a moment about you. What do you do? Are you a CEO, manager, entrepreneur, top person on the totem pole, or brand new to the company? Are you a consultant, author, teacher, speaker, doctor, lawyer, idea person, scientist, or inventor? Whoever you are, you have a label. Whether you are employed in your dream career or in search of what will put you on the map, your success depends on what you think minute by minute, inkling by inkling. To achieve success, you have to plant a seed of greatness.

From this point forward, you must nurture that seed into a vision of success. And by this we mean *Wow* success–greater success than you ever dreamed possible. Well, maybe you *have* dreamed of it, but so far you haven't achieved it. For a variety of reasons, you haven't truly gotten started, or you've made a couple of failed attempts or maybe you've even enjoyed a bit of success but not nearly as much as you want.

Or perhaps you've achieved far more than you ever dreamed possible and find yourself ready to raise the bar to even greater heights. Whatever your experience, whatever your background, you can reach and even surpass the level of success you've imagined by following the 16-step process in this book, and that means starting right here with the first law of *Wow* marketing: *Envision your success.*

※ WHAT DO YOU HAVE IN COMMON WITH A SWEET POTATO QUEEN?

Your initial idea or business plan for growing your company doesn't have to come to you in grand and glorious Technicolor. It can start with just a vague sense of what you want and love to do. This is the way it started for Jill Conner Browne, whose Sweet Potato Queens "empire" includes *New York Times* best-selling, megamemorable novels and kitchy merchandise targeted to middle-class, middle-aged women who have created more than 5,000 Sweet Potato Queen chapters throughout the world. Imagine organizing one fan-loving, book-reading following for yourself or your company and then multiplying it by over 5,000. We think that's a lot of supporters and ultimately customers.

The cornerstone event for the organization is an annual parade held in Browne's hometown of Jackson, Mississippi. The Sweet Potato Queens appear resplendent in wild and crazy wigs and costumes—a fashion statement that screams uniqueness—designed for laughs and outrageous self-expression. Browne started out doing it only for fun, but she recalls a moment during the first parade in 1982, years before she established the business, when she knew that she was onto something.

"The first time I rode in the pickup truck, enthusiastically waving to the crowd, declaring myself as the Sweet Potato Queen, I said, 'Someday, someone will pay me to do this,' she says. "I always thought this was the most fun I ever had, and if it entertained me, it would entertain others. I had no plan at all. I just wanted to be in a parade to entertain myself."

From that first thought, she built a business that easily qualifies as a *Wow* success. Although she had no plan for how to build the joy and happiness she felt during the parade into a lucrative business, she had taken her first step on the path toward achieving her goal. In that moment, she had her first vision of success, which, to her, was much more about doing something fun that would entertain her and many others than about making a lot of money.

"For me, success is measured by my level of satisfaction in what I'm doing," Browne told us. "I'm happy to be financially successful, but that's not the most important thing. I'm satanically lazy. I don't want to do anything at all. I don't even like to do errands. If it feels like work to me, if I don't love it, I won't do it. It seems like everyone should be that way, and they're not."

While Jill Conner Browne might call herself lazy, we call her ingenious in that she found a way to pay her bills and become a best-selling author, entertainer, and comedian, and true to her "big hair" rhinestone-covered tiara, this beloved icon created a following around the world. Not bad for a banner-covered woman in a pickup truck who just wanted to wear a crown. We love Jill Conner Browne's humor and honesty, two key qualities in what has made her so successful. We can, however, echo her belief in starting with what you love to do.

"When I talk to people about finding your own personal happiness, I tell them that to find it, think about what you did as a child, what did you do for fun on your own," she says. "I loved to read and write, and I loved to play dress up. Look at that, and it will inform you."

People have taken a lot of different roads to *Wow* success, but they all share one key quality—*passion*. Passion must fuel your vision of success. You've got to feel passionate about what you're doing in order to achieve your goal. If your idea doesn't excite you, you won't be able to excite customers about it. If your idea doesn't excite you, any success you manage to achieve will be measured only in dollars. The sacrifices and commitment required to reach the success you envision will seem like drudgery. If you love your idea and the plan that it inspires, however, your excitement and energy will become contagious.

☀ SEEING IS BELIEVING

Creating an idea that excites you, however, is just the first step. With this idea clearly in mind, you have to envision your success. Not everyone stops to think about what success looks like for them, but understanding what lights your fire, what makes you feel alive and connected, and what makes you want to get up in the morning and take on the world is important. You have to mold and shape it in your mind, and you have to believe that you can make it happen. Success always requires commitment and often requires a certain amount of risk. It demands that we conquer the doubts and fears that inevitably plague us as we move forward with a new idea. In the famous words of pitcher Tug McGraw of the pennant-winning 1973 New York Mets, "Ya gotta believe."

The best way to foster such belief is by visualizing it. Some people visualize simply by closing their eyes and meditating on images of their success. Others write down their vision on paper. Still others say it out loud to themselves, developing what amounts to a success mantra.

As Doug Hall says in his book, *The Maverick Mindset*, "Once you see it, you can be it." Hall began his career developing and marketing products for Proctor & Gamble and then launched his own company, The Eureka Ranch, where many Fortune 500 companies go to create new ideas for products and services. For visualizing your success, Hall recommends a three-step process: (1) See yourself enjoying the fruits of your success, (2) walk yourself backward to your current situation and note each step along the way, and (3) move forward by taking your first step. He says, "The key to your journey is feeling in your heart that you've already arrived before you started."

Experiment with various ways to visualize your success and find the one that works for you. And then do it regularly enough that the vision is clear and fresh in your mind. Return to it often. In his book, *Win Every Day*, college football coach turned television analyst and motivational speaker Lou Holtz suggests beginning every day by declaring one positive step that you'll take to achieve your long-range goal. See yourself taking that step and thereby reaching your goal by successfully taking the smaller steps toward it.

Whichever method you use, the key is keeping your vision clear. Once you begin your journey to *Wow* success, there will be many bumps along the way, times of being unsure which way to turn, and even times when you'll wonder if you're crazy for thinking that you can do what you've set out to do. Your vision of success will guide you, bolster you, and nurture you through these times, a beacon lighting your way.

☀ COME AS YOU'LL BE

Jack Canfield, along with his partner Mark Victor Hansen, has built a hugely successful business through his famous *Chicken Soup* books. There are more than 100 million copies in print worldwide, and the pair holds the record for most books on the *New York Times*' best-seller list at one time—seven, in 1998. Both are popular motivational speakers and workshop leaders.

To help people envision success, Canfield holds a party that he calls "Come as You'll Be." Guests dress up to be who they'll be in five years, after they've achieved their goals.

"I've had guys dressed up as Hugh Hefner," Canfield says. "I've had guys show up in tuxedo, as if they just won the Oscar. I once had a young man walking around with a cell phone saying, "J. Lo, it's over." By dressing up as they want to be, guests take the first step in making it happen. They literally envision their success—in the mirror.

"It has an internal effect on the subconscious," Canfield explains. "When you start visualizing and feeling strongly about what you want, you move toward it. We want to program that subconscious mind with strong images of success. It's like a GPS system. If I really see myself thin, now I have a destination in there, and the subconscious starts charting a way to get there."

The effect, however, is not only internal.

"On an external level, through the law of attraction, your thoughts can travel around the earth. When you think a thought, it travels through space. It will attract people who are aligned with the goals you want to achieve."

Canfield cites a case in point. He and Hansen set a goal of selling 1 million books in a single day. They visualized the goal and talked about it and looked for ways to make it happen. A month later, they attended Book Expo America, the large annual convention for publishers, and Canfield was sitting on the shuttle from the convention center to the hotel after a long day. A woman sat down next to him and introduced herself as a buyer for a national bookstore chain. They chatted for a bit, and Canfield mentioned the goal of selling a million books in a day.

The idea sparked the woman's interest. She began to formulate a plan for appearances at airports throughout the country, traveling from the East to West to many cities in a single day.

"I asked her why she would be willing to help us reach our goal," Canfield recalls with a laugh. "She said, 'Dummy, if I sold a million books in one day, don't you think that would make me look good?' Some people would say that's lucky. But when you send out your thought with certainty, you attract the people who can help you."

So maybe the first step on your path to *Wow* success is to throw a party. Put yourself and who you want to know on the guest list. Put together a vision for who you want to be in five years, and put yourself on the guest list (and you thought this was going to be difficult).

 SHAPING YOUR VISION

But wait, as the "infomercialers" love to say, there's more. You're not yet finished envisioning your success. To this point, we've focused on how you feel about your vision—feeling passionate and believing that you can succeed. Now we turn to the practical aspects of your vision, the nuts and bolts of it. The next step in envisioning your success requires you to be more specific. You have to envision how you're going to reach your destination, moving from mental images to a plan for turning those images into reality. Without envisioning a plan, you run the risk of wandering around in the dark, grabbing at every opportunity that appears along the way in the hope that it will lead to where you want to be.

You need a clear and specific vision that will help you to make the right decisions. We've looked at where you'll be in five years, but you need to plot how you're going to make that happen. Where do you want to be in three months, six months, a year? Step back and assess each of those points along the way. None of us can see into the future, but you can determine if the steps you've outlined ultimately will lead to your goal. You can determine if achieving the intermediary goals is possible, if you're overreaching or moving too slowly, if you're counting on factors over which you have little control, or ideally, if you can, with hard work and a focused approach, be right where you need to be at each step along the way.

Let's continue developing your vision of success. Remember to be as specific as possible at this stage. Consider: Who are your customers? How will you reach them? What primary need are you filling? How large a business do you want to build? How many employees will you need? How much money will you make? We'll cover each of these elements in later chapters, but it already should be clear that they all work together.

Right now, you may have only a vague idea of what you want to accomplish—wealth, freedom to travel, a successful business to pass on to your children—and that's fine. But don't try to move forward until you've got a more developed vision of the success you want to achieve. Stated in the most basic way: Without a clear understanding of your destination, you're far less likely to reach it.

"When we were writing *Chicken Soup*, we said, 'We're writing a best-selling book,'" recalls Jack Canfield. "We never doubted for a minute that we would sell the book."

And that vision remained intact despite nearly 150 rejections. They were told that the title was stupid, that people no longer read short stories, and that the message was too positive. But they kept their vision clear and used it as a guiding light during the storm of nay-sayers. Your vision can sustain you in the times when you wonder if you're on the right track and if you'll ever realize your dream.

☀ PAINTING A PICTURE

Some business people say that envisioning your success isn't neces-sary, that fooling about with mission statements and visions can be a way of delaying the first step. Although there is a certain validity to the sug-gestion that many people's dreams of success remain little more than dreams, we believe in creating a vision. In our experience, when we've begun with a vision and developed the specific steps toward achieving it, we've enjoyed much greater success than if we'd simply jumped in feet first.

Saying that you want to be successful or famous or a best-seller or a Fortune 100 company doesn't cut it. Sure, you want that huge, global success. But you have to boil it down to something specific. Paint a brighter picture and describe the details—the brush strokes, the colors, the subject matter. Envision clearly what you want.

Tom Watson, Sr., founder of IBM, agrees. In Michael Gerber's *The E-Myth Revisited*, Watson states:

IBM is what it is today for three special reasons. The first reason is that, at the very beginning, I had a very clear picture of what the company would look like when it was finally done. You might say I had a model in my mind of what it would look like when the dream—my vision—was in place.

The second reason was that once I had that picture, I then asked myself how a company which looked like that would have to act. I then created a picture of how IBM would act when it was finally done.

The third reason IBM has been so successful was that once I had a picture of how IBM would look like when the dream was in place and how such a company would have to act, I then realized that, unless we began to act that way from the very beginning, we would never get there.

In other words, I realized that for IBM to become a great company, it would have to act like a great company long before it ever became one.

Your vision may not be to build a business the size and scope of IBM, but your vision should be one of achieving greatness—of achieving *Wow* success. Who dreams of only a little success? To sum up: Aim high, envision that lofty place, believe that you can get there, and create a plan for doing it.

Read on! And let us help you define and arrive at your most determined destination. ✳

CHAPTER 2

You Gotta Have a "Brand Slam"!

> Products are made in the factory, but brands are created in the mind.
>
> —**Walter Landor**

As you develop your marketing plan, ask yourself about your brand. For a number of years now, *brand* and *branding* have been buzzwords in the world of marketing. Much of what we hear about branding is couched in "marketing speak," which often means that it has a great sense of urgency but doesn't make a whole lot of sense. At least it doesn't seem like something you can apply in clear, practical terms to your situation, service, or product.

So we'll take our own advice and "Keep it simple."

Your brand is the way your customers view you, the sum total of what they think about when they think about you (or your product or service). The brand embodies their expectations, which are based on their experiences as well as on the marketing messages you give them. If you provide a benefit to them by solving a problem, they will see you as a valuable ally. Proctor & Gamble (P&G), the world's leading manufacturer of household cleansers, calls one of its Web sites "Everyday Solutions" to increase its customers' belief that P&G provides answers to their questions and solutions to their problems.

BusinessWeek magazine and the Interbrand Agency produce an annual report ranking the top 100 global brands in the world, applying strict criteria for measuring the strength and value of the brands. The number one global brand, according to the report, is Coca-Cola, followed by Microsoft, IBM, General Electric, and Intel. Disney and McDonald's also made the top 10.

These are huge companies, of course, and their strength is based in part on the amount of money they spend on advertising. They keep themselves in front of us. You probably aren't operating on quite so large a scale, but the point we're making is that customers know and trust these brands. When customers think of Coca-Cola, or Microsoft, or Disney, they have specific reactions. To understand those reactions, consider your own. Or make your own top 10 list of brands. Which ones inspire trust? Which ones make you feel good about life and yourself? Which ones do you admire? Ask yourself why you feel this way. Have you had positive experiences with them? Have their marketing messages captured your attention, your heart, and your loyalty?

When you finish your list, consider another–this time list the brands that you don't trust or admire, that don't make you feel good. Think about why you feel this way. Have you had bad experiences with these brands or know someone who has suffered bad experiences with them? Try to pinpoint what you don't like and why. Your reactions, both positive and negative, will help you to understand the nature of your own brand.

The best way to think about branding is that it's your identity in the minds of consumers. It's what they think about when they think about you.

✳ YOU: THE BRAND

To begin building your brand, begin with yourself. In terms of your marketing campaign, as well as your career goals, *you* are a brand. Your customers–and colleagues and associates–have opinions about you. They have expectations based on previous experience as well as on what they've heard about you (whether or not what they've heard is true).

It's probably easier to understand how people are brands if we look at public figures. Politicians are brands. Hillary Clinton, for example, projects different views, beliefs, and personal qualities than George Bush projects. Both are brands. Paris Hilton is just as much a brand as Google or Pepsi. When we hear of her latest exploits, we have expectations as well as preconceived notions, opinions, and feelings. Do you find yourself saying, "Paris is outrageous! I love her."? Or are you saying, "Now, tell me again why she's famous."?

As you develop your personal brand, you'll want to make it as positive as possible, of course. And you'll want to strive to be consistent. When you've developed positive feelings for your brand, you want to maintain those feelings. If your customer is confused by the brand, isn't sure what to expect from it, the customer's interest (and trust and loyalty) will weaken.

In his book, *You Are the Message*, former television producer Roger Ailes recalls meeting comedian Jack Benny for the first time. When they met, Benny was an old man, a legend in the entertainment business, but long past his prime. Ailes says he was stunned that Benny, who would be a guest that day on a live show Ailes was producing, looked so old and frail. Benny was hunched over and spoke in a whisper. The show, Ailes feared, would be a disaster. "I thought, 'Oh my God, he's going to pass away right on the air today,'" Ailes writes. Jack Benny was a brand. His audience knew him and had very definite expectations of him. Benny was wry and smooth and made jokes about his tight-fisted nature. It appeared that the Benny brand was in for a change. Ailes was stunned, however, when the old man, right before going on stage, went through an amazing transformation.

"Benny inhaled and energy seemed to enter his body," Ailes writes. "I swear he grew an entire foot. He looked twenty-five years younger. He looked at me, smiled and winked, and as the doors opened for his entrance, he broke into his famous arm-swinging stride and walked on stage."

Now that's protecting a brand! Benny knew what his audience expected, what they loved about him, and he delivered it. This is more than just a "show must go on" story. It's about understanding what people want from you and giving it to them, time and again, despite whatever obstacles appear in your way.

If you provide reliable service, customers will come to you when they need that service. Whether you've developed a new stain remover or written funny newspaper columns or established yourself as the go-to person at your office, you've established a brand identity that you'll want to understand—and protect—at all costs.

As you develop your marketing campaign, think about your brand—even if you're still in the early stages of developing it. How will your customers perceive the brand? How will it make them feel? What emotions will it elicit from them? What are its strengths and weaknesses?

To put it even more simply, your brand means how your customers perceive you. What do they expect from you, your product, or your service? Do they have an emotional response, and is it a good one?

✳ MAKING A DIFFERENCE

David D'Alessandro is the former chairman and CEO of John Hancock Life Insurance Company and is the author of the best-selling book *Brand Warfare*. He believes that brands are crucial in differentiating products in the marketplace—especially when the actual differences between the products are not significant enough for the typical consumer to notice.

Case in point: Before taking on the position at John Hancock, D'Alessandro worked for years in marketing agencies, and he worked on the campaign for Orville Redenbacher Gourmet Popcorn during the product's introduction to the marketplace.

"At the time, popcorn wasn't branded," he says. "You bought it in a generic plastic bag or in those aluminum pans. And the fact is, most popcorn is pretty much the same. One isn't very different from the other. The difference is really just in your head. But Orville Redenbacher took what I had grown up to see as a generic food, and he made it something you really had to have. What I came to realize was that people want to buy brands they're comfortable with. The world of branding to a great extent is what David Copperfield does for a living—it's an illusion."

But making your brand distinct and making it something people must have are crucial. And that requires establishing a distinction and establishing trust. D'Alessandro says the key to establishing and maintaining that trust is consistency.

"When you have decided on a marketing direction for whatever brand, do not change," he says. "It may not be working right away, and there will be enormous pressure on you, but if you have done your work properly, do not change. You must have faith that you've done the work up front—and you have to do that work. When you start changing your strategy in midstream, you so confuse the marketplace and your distributors, your product, or career, goes down the tubes. I've seen so many products that panic. There aren't that many products that will give you instant gratification. But once you start, don't turn around."

※ DOES BRAND MATTER?

In a word, *Yes.* Your brand is your identity in the marketplace. You may not think that it's who you really are, but, believe us, customers do think this way.

"Many people casually assume they are brands and then go about living their business lives as if brands don't really matter," says Laura Ries, a leading brand consultant, best-selling author, sought-after speaker, and media personality frequently featured on CNN, Fox News, CNBC, ABC, and CBS. She is president of Ries & Ries Consulting and has coauthored with her father, Al Ries, several branding classics, including *The 22 Immutable Laws of Branding, The Fall of Advertising & the Rise of PR,* and *The Origin of Brands.* "Brands do matter. Brands are what enable you to make profits. If you don't have a brand, then you have a commodity, and everybody knows there is no money in selling commodities."

Ries says the key to building a brand effectively is to focus on what you do well and then to build your identity around that quality. "When you ask most people what they are good at, they usually reply, 'I'm good with people, I'm a good planner and organizer, and I'm good at strategic thinking,'" she explains. "Translation: I'm good at everything. Is that any way to build a brand? No, you build a brand by narrowing the focus and becoming a specialist." The key to brand-building success is finding one *Wow* trait about yourself and building your brand around it. Unlike dollars, too many *Wows* is no good.

✳ WHAT'S IN A NAME?

Laura believes that one of the most important elements in your brand is your name. In the minds of consumers, your name *is* your brand. It's the way consumers know you, identify you, and remember you. It must be memorable, and you must do everything possible to protect it.

"If you don't have a good brand name, what would you do if you considered yourself a brand?" she asks. "Obviously, you would change it. The name is the hook that hangs your brand on the product ladder in the prospect's mind. The single most important marketing decision you can make is what to name a product or yourself. When Ralph Lifshitz wanted to become a famous designer, he didn't start by working 24 hours a day designing clothes. The first thing he did was change his name to Ralph Lauren. Ralph could have been the best darn designer in the world, but he wouldn't have gotten anywhere as a designer unless he first got rid of the Lifshitz. What is a brand anyhow? It's not necessarily a better product or person, although it may be. A brand stands for something and owns a word or category in the mind of the prospect. Volvo and safety. Starbucks and coffee. Google and search. Paris and heiress. Julia Roberts and pretty woman. Arnold Schwarzenegger and terminator—now governator."

Laura articulates this marketing truth very well, but the idea didn't originate with her. In some ways we've always known it, if only subconsciously. Savvy marketers certainly have been conscious of it for years. In her memoir,

Laughing with Lucy, Madelyn Pugh Davis, who wrote or oversaw the writing of scripts for all of Lucille Ball's TV shows, recalls a word that was forbidden.

"When *I Love Lucy* first went on the air, our sponsor was Philip Morris cigarettes," she writes. "We were requested not to use the word 'lucky' in a script because one of their big competitors was Lucky Strike, so we would say someone was 'fortunate.' It took me years to get over feeling guilty when I said 'lucky.'" The sponsor knew the power of a name and wasn't about to have a big star like Lucy exclaiming it to millions of people when she got a lucky break. (Not that Lucy Ricardo got many of them.) So even 50 years later, when you watch the classic reruns, you won't hear about anyone feeling "lucky."

The story illustrates the power of a name.

In Carl Hamilton's book, *Absolut: Biography of a Bottle*, we read about the steps that are sometimes taken to arrive at a brand name. The owners and ad folks worked through a whole litany of names, such as The Country of Sweden Vodka, The Blond Swede, Royal Court Vodka, Damn Swede, Explorer Vodka, and Absolute Pure Vodka, among others. The last one remained a favorite among the creative group because it implied the benefit—that other vodkas might be pure, but this was the purest. But it was a long name, so they shortened it to Absolute Vodka. Finally, they agreed on the Swedish spelling of the word, which they felt would draw more interest. By dropping the *e*, they would force the American consumer to subconsciously complete the spelling. "By leaving that little opening, you slyly involved them in the creative process," Hamilton writes. "They were claiming to have created the ultimate vodka, and now they were going to flat out say so—whether it was in good taste or not. Absolut without the *e* was more cunning. Absolut was more absolute than Absolute."

Nearly 30 years later, the name is famous and has been used in the product's pithy two-word ads, "Absolut [fill in the blank]," for years. It should be noted that while the name and packaging discussions were raging on and on, not a single drop of vodka had been produced. Absolut was branded as the absolutely most pure vodka before the product actually had been made.

Wally Amos had one of the most recognized names in the cookie aisle of your grocery store, but he no longer is able to use it. "Famous Amos" is still a very popular brand of cookies, but Wally hasn't been involved in the brand (now owned by Kellogg) since the early 1990s. Unfortunately, when he lost the company, he also lost access to his own name. He is now a shareholder in and spokesperson for Uncle Wally's Muffin Company and is doing his best to spread the word that Uncle Wally and Famous Amos are one in the same. Wally Amos might have lost the ability to use his Famous Amos name, but he never lost his contagious passion or his vision or love for a great-tasting product, which remains the core of his brand.

"We realize the value in Wally Amos as a brand," Amos said in an Associated Press article by Lucy Pemoni. "Our goal is to let the public know that Uncle Wally is Wally Amos."

✳ GET EMOTIONAL

The marketing experts agree that the most successful brands inspire an emotional response from their customers. This response usually goes beyond simply the acknowledged benefit the brand provides. The brand produces a deeper reaction tied to the customers' emotions. In *Fast Food Nation*, Eric Schlosser wrote about how McDonald's uses its Playland area to hardwire happy, positive emotions in children so that when they grow up, they'll retain that unconscious feeling about the brand. More than a lure for kids to nag their parents into stopping for lunch, McDonald's Playland creates a resonance that the company hopes will last a lifetime.

Another beloved brand, according to myriad surveys, is Gerber baby food. For many people it's one of their earliest memories. The baby on the jar attracts their attention when they are being fed, and a warm feeling is instilled in them. When those babies have babies of their own, they'll choose the Gerber brand.

Most brands, however, struggle to engender and retain that emotional response. And unfortunately, it's a fact of life that negative emotions are evoked more easily than positive ones. A bad experience–poor service, unreliable or inadequate resolution of complaints–can make a customer feel a negative reaction that is very difficult to dislodge. This is why it's so difficult to change a customer's mind once it's made up–the feeling is more in the heart than the mind.

A classic attempt is Ford Motor Company's slogan, "Have you driven a Ford, lately?" Implied in the message is that the vehicles and service are far better than they used to be. The hope is that we'll give them another chance.

✳ HALLMARK OR HOBGOBLIN?

To retain positive feelings and loyal repeat purchases, brands work hard to remain consistent. As David D'Alessandro pointed out earlier in this chapter, a brand that constantly changes its identity confuses consumers. Such brands make us think, "Who are they? What do they stand for? Can they be trusted?" Consistency may be the "hobgoblin of little minds," but it's the hallmark of successful brands.

The most famous case of the importance of consistency is Coca-Cola's decision in 1985 to change its recipe and introduce New Coke–which led to a huge backlash from consumers, so huge that the company quickly brought back its original product under the name Coca-Cola Classic.

As you develop your own brand, work hard to understand its identity, its appeal to the market you want to reach. Seek to make an emotional connection with your customers.

How do you want your customers to feel about your brand? Financial institutions, for example, tend to promote trust and peace of mind. For years,

State Farm Insurance has used the slogan, "And like a good neighbor, State Farm is there."

Consider everything that you must do to hit your brand out of the ballpark, reaching fans forever. But don't assume success—success is a never-ending journey. And when you've made it, do everything it takes to maintain those positive feelings. Maintain a clear connection with your audience, and make sure that the laws of *Wow* are being exercised and practiced daily.

So ask yourself what your brand stands for. Can you sum it up in a few words? One word? Your brand must slam a thought into the public mind and must stay there. It must be memorable. If you stand for everything, you stand for nothing. To accentuate your brand, you must bond with the consumer on a higher level.

CREATING A BRAND STATEMENT

Margo Berman is an award-winning creativity expert, professor, inventor, trainer, and author of *Street-Smart Advertising: How to Win the Battle of the Buzz*. She is president of Creative Catalyst Unlock the Block and an associate professor of advertising at Florida International University. She offers the following tips for creating a brand statement that customers will remember:

1. *Put your company name in slogan.* You think that this is obvious, but it's not. Look how Smucker's leveraged its name in the slogan, "With a name like Smucker's, it has to be good." The audience was reminded about what could have been a deficit. With Aflac, the company quacked the name, making it instantly sticky.

2. *Use rhyme.* "Fill it to the rim with Brim." "Before you dress, Caress."

3. *Employ alliteration.* Reuse the same first sound. Look how easy "Do the Dew" is to remember.

4. *Try a play on words.* This is a lighthearted approach, such as Planters' line, "Relax. Go Nuts."

5. *Include parallel construction.* Repeat a word or phrase. Look how long Doublemint's slogan hangs in your mind: "Double your pleasure. Double your fun. Doublemint, Doublemint, Doublemint gum." How about the Meow Mix jingle, which repeats the name over and over again?

6. *Combine some techniques.* Notice how the Brim (number 2 above) uses the name in the rhyme.

7. *Use vernacular or everyday speech.* Checkers line, "You gotta eat," states the obvious in a familiar tone.

8. *Challenge the audience.* Everyone knows how this Lay's Baked Potato Chip tagline works: "Betcha can't eat just one."

9. *Try a command, without sounding bossy.* When Nike created "Just do it," it didn't tell you what to do. Just do whatever you like.

10. *Explain your promise or purpose.* General Electric states, "Imagination at work."

11. *Ask a simple question.* Think about, "Got Milk?" Then the campaign showed humorous milk-deprivation scenarios.

12. *Use simile.* Include *like* or *as*, for instance, Chevy's "Like a Rock."

13. *Explain the reason why to buy.* The number one slogan of the century (according to *Ad Age*) is DeBeers' line, "A diamond is forever."

14. *Consider onomatopoeia* (where the word sounds like it is). Alka-Seltzer could never be confused with any other product: "Plop. Plop. Fizz. Fizz." The line even continues with a (rhymed) promise: "Oh, what a relief it is."

15. *Apply emotional blackmail to make the audience feel anxious.* "Raise your hand if you're Sure." How sure are you that your deodorant is working?

16. *Try a testimonial.* "I coulda had a V8!" This slogan also uses vernacular and name, as does "L'Oréal. I'm worth it."

It should be clear from all these examples that there is not a magic formula for creating your "brand slam" statement, but keep these ideas in mind if you want to own the mindshare of your brand. ✳

CHAPTER 3

Find Your Unique Edge—and Sharpen It

The best way to have a good idea is to have lots of ideas.

—Linus Pauling

Anyone in marketing knows that to be successful, you have to have some type of unique selling proposition to break through the noise and call attention to yourself and your idea. As you know by now, we call that quality your *Wow*.

Your *Wow* must be clear and appealing—and quickly understood. It makes your brand, product, or service more recognizable and distinctive, which is more important than ever, given the many other marketing messages bombarding customers in our mediacentric age. A recent report by the 3M Company states that the average American adult is exposed to more than 3,000 marketing messages per day! You need to have an edge to cut through the clutter and truly stand out.

✳ SELLING THE BROOKLYN BRIDGE

No story exemplifies sharpening your edge better than one involving marketing guru and well-known businessman Paul Hartunian. In a nutshell, Paul was watching television one day and saw a story on the news about a work crew who had pulled up the weather-beaten walkway from the actual Brooklyn Bridge. Paul called the guy who was hauling the wood away and told him he would pay $500 to have the wood delivered to him. Then he immediately arranged for the wood to be taken to a lumberyard and cut up into tiny pieces.

Paul then sent a press release to hundreds of media outlets with the headline, "New Jersey Man Sells the Brooklyn Bridge—$14.95 plus Shipping." He took one of the best-known jokes in the world and made millions selling it from just one press release. By having an edge, he tapped into the enormous powers of major media and ended up appearing on *The Tonight Show* and reaching millions of people around the world.

Mailing those press releases cost Paul less than $100 and triggered a flood of newspaper and magazine reporters, as well as radio and TV shows, providing him with publicity that reached a huge audience over the course of a few months. CNN sent a truck to his front door, interviewed him, and ran that interview every half hour for three days. Not only did Johnny Carson promote his product on the show, but he also put together one of his special parodies based on the product. Paul appeared on *To Tell the Truth, The Regis Philbin Show,* and more than a thousand radio and TV shows throughout the United States and in several other countries. A two-page article about him appeared in *Forbes* magazine.

"Woody Allen said 80 percent of success is showing up," Hartunian says. "The idea of the Brooklyn Bridge was probably my 1140th idea. I appreciate when people say you're a marketing genius, but the truth is I tried so many ideas, and most of my ideas before that didn't make it. The Brooklyn Bridge was a homerun, but everyone can hit one out of the park. It's all about people showing up without excuses. Don't give up sounds cliché, but it's absolutely true. Thomas Edison tried ten thousand ways to make a lightbulb and failed until that final time. When asked about all the times he failed, Edison replied, 'I didn't fail. Now I know ten thousand ways not to make a lightbulb.'

"In essence, I did the same thing and used Edison's principle. I never want people to think this could only happen to Paul Hartunian. There's hope for everyone on this planet to do their Brooklyn Bridge."

✴ ROBYN FINDS HER EDGE

As a leading consumer advocate and one of the country's foremost gift and product experts, I've appeared on local and national media, from over 25 years on WXIA, the NBC affiliate, to my *Giftionary* radio show based on my books, *The Giftionary* and *Make It Memorable*, on Star 94 (www.star94.com) in Atlanta with Cindy and Ray, to multiple appearances on CNN, *Headline News*, national talk shows such as *The Today Show*, and extensively in national magazines and newspapers across America. If I can end up on national television and reach millions of consumers through my love and knowledge of shopping, I always say that you can accomplish anything!

In 1981, after teaching art for a handful of years and being a full-time, devoted elementary school teacher, I retired from teaching when my first child, Justin, who is now 27 and an attorney, was born. I became a stay-at-home mom, writing books, and I wanted to be the best mom and parent I could possibly be. However, I never viewed myself as retired. Rather, I was inspired to put my talents and gifts—my *Wow*—to work. As a newly published author of a how-to craft book and also an educational book for teachers, I made an appearance on the local NBC affiliate in Atlanta and became a how-to expert on Atlanta's leading talk show called *Noonday*. I ended up appearing on that show twice a week for 16 years. Along the way, as I wrote and coauthored many books on topics such as parenting, entertaining, kids, and gift giving, I built a recognizable and credible name as a parenting expert, super mom, and ultimately, the "Super Shopper" on WXIA-TV. As time continued, I was interviewed by many national newspapers and magazines and even started writing for many of them.

The key was to build bridges along the way, offering helpful information that made people smarter, better, and brighter, which became my motto. I never rested on my laurels. I paid attention to trends, news you could use, and things that also truly mattered most to me as a mom. However, I never wasted time letting someone else define the trends. If something appealed to me and other moms in Atlanta, I trusted my judgment and knew enough to know what would appeal to my viewers.

After studying the marketplace, I realized that there weren't many, if even any, shopping experts in the local media at the time. (This was well before the current array of home shopping shows, especially in Atlanta.) I wanted to know where to shop, smart ways to save money, and fabulous places to spend my money wisely, and I worked diligently to find that information.

It's important to be an authority in your own backyard first, and that's a great way to build your craft, talents, and skills. It's all about knowing what stands out and hollers fabulous. One thing I've always said is that "America doesn't need another same old, same old." I did whatever was necessary to make myself unique and to create an edge of originality that would interest people and get them buzzing. Now, more than 26 years later, I reach millions of readers, listeners, and viewers and over the years have created a platform that I work hard to maintain. I show up and try to make a place better than I found it. I want to bring something meaningful to my work and never rest on my laurels. I suppose that's why I love writing books, and it's embedded in my soul as a teacher to want to inspire others to succeed, to be meaningful gift givers, to be better parents, and to make every moment memorable.

☀ A TOY STORY

When Mattel toy designer Roger Sweet created the He-Man action figure, nothing quite like it had ever been done before. In 1976, Mattel had decided against paying for the licensing contract to produce the action figures for a soon-to-be-released science fiction movie titled, *Star Wars*, which went on to stunning success. Hasbro had locked up the military action figure back in the 1960s with G.I. Joe. Mattel needed a winner.

The initial idea, says Sweet, occurred to him while he was studying the muscular barbarians in the illustrations of Frank Frazetta. He also was trying to develop a figure that was not subject to any single space or time because the competition had already laid claim to two of the most popular figures. He needed a figure that instantly would draw the attention of boys and would allow them to put that figure in any play scenario that tickled their imagination at any time.

Sweet had been toying (pardon the pun) with a Viking-type figure called *Vykon* that was the first to have the huge muscles that later would make He-Man such an original. But Vykon was limited and lacked the striking originality Sweet was trying to create. He continued to expand and refine his idea, ultimately creating a figure in three separate guises, all of which would be called *He-Man*. Each had the massive, ripped body that Sweet knew would attract attention. He molded the figure into a crouched stance with arms bent, as if ready to take on the world, another departure from the action figures of the time, which were always designed to stand straight.

"My little man plastic man would be generic but heroic, with huge, massively exaggerated, incredibly well-defined muscles," Sweet recalls. "I thought it would be compelling because what boy doesn't dream of having the kinds of muscles that make people draw back in awe? What I had in mind was a radical departure from anything that had come before in the world of male action figures."

Though he admits to being nervous about such a "radical departure," Sweet was right about how boys would respond. They'd never seen anything like it, and there was no doubt in their minds that their army of action figures just got a new champion. During the six-year heyday of He-Man, the line earned $1.2 billion worldwide.

✴ STAR POWER

Defining the qualities of a *Wow* isn't easy. If there were a recipe with all the necessary ingredients listed for you, it would be a lot easier. Then again, it wouldn't be as special. Sometimes determining what makes a *Wow* is like the old joke about knowing what type of art you like—you know it when you see it.

Scott Wine is a partner at The Osbrink Agency, a company that has grown into a prestigious, full-service agency providing the entertainment and fashion industries with many of the most visible clients in film, television, commercials, voice-overs, and print. To select the right clients for his agency, Wine needs to be able to recognize a *Wow* when he sees one.

"Being an agent is a very unique and special job," he says. "We have the opportunity to make dreams come true. I feel like we get a handful of magic dust, and it is our job to find the right people to bestow it upon. I can tell in about six seconds flat if someone has that special *je ne sais quoi*. I love some-one that has a burning desire to prove something—someone whose feet just seem to tap and whose hands seem to feel their way through a room. You shake their hand and you feel like they are your new best friend. Their charisma makes them special. They illuminate a room just by their presence and light.

"I always look for an individual who seems to have an old soul, which we consider to be the prodigy of all prodigies. They seem like they have traveled this landscape for a hundred years, but they just learned how to walk. It's remarkable. Their magnetism makes you want to watch them. You are drawn to them. They are natural storytellers that keep you wanting more. They know how to work a room. Their competitive passion transforms rejection. The word 'no' only means NOT NOW. The word 'mediocre' does not exist in their vernacular. We may imagine this quality to be magic, but it is business and big business at that. There is no room for the 'NORM' as it could not coexist amongst the giants!"

✸ DECIDE WHO YOU ARE—AND THEN GO PLAY

We grabbed the title of this section from advice we received from Marissa Mayer, a vice president at Google. In our discussion with her, she said that there's more than one way to launch an idea. In fact, she said, "There are two ways. You can be a castle-builder, where you go behind the curtain, build your castle in secrecy, and when it's ready, you announce it with tons of fanfare—or you can launch early and often and let the market tell you where to go. For the more timid or humble, or when the market is rapidly changing, launch early and often works best. But you have to decide who you are."

Mayer leads the product management efforts on Google's search products—Web search, product search, images, groups, news, the Google Toolbar, Google Desktop, Google Labs, and more. She joined the Google staff of 18 people in 1999 as the company's first female engineer. At that time, she led the user interface and Web server teams. Now, with over 15,000 employees, Google is a worldwide phenomenon. Mayer's successes have included designing and developing Google's search interface; internationalizing the site to more than 100 languages; defining Google News, Gmail, and Orkut; and launching more than 100 features and products on Google.com. Several patents have been filed on her work in artificial intelligence and interface design. She also has taught introductory computer programming classes at Stanford to over 3,000 students, and Stanford recognized her with the Centennial Teaching Award and the Forsythe Award for her outstanding contribution to undergraduate education. She has been featured in various publications, including *Newsweek* ("10 Tech Leaders of the Future"), *Red Herring* ("15 Women to Watch"), *Business 2.0* ("Silicon Valley Dream Team"), *BusinessWeek*, *Fortune*, and *Fast Company*. In short, just like Google, Marissa Mayer is a *Wow*. She's launched enough products to speak with experience and expertise.

"Google launches early and often, and lets the market tell us where to go," she says. "Users go behind the curtain with us, and help us adapt. Users are ultimately the powerful and helpful indicators for what you should do next. When you launch early and often, you launch, but you move a little bit and you don't end up too far off the line. The market pulls you back on vector. Even if you veer off, the market and users give you feedback. You have much more communication with your users. You might not get the same wow effect, but you do get results.

"Castle builders by definition are comfortable with higher risk. They're behind the curtains and suddenly emerge with a working program. They are confident and know they are building the right thing, even if it takes years. Castle building has a strong *Wow* effect, but the downside is you don't know your market as well, and that's when you can get a dud of enormous proportions. Huge reward when the market responds favorably to it. Huge risk if they don't."

As you're developing your idea, Mayer adds, don't ignore the power of play. She and her colleagues at Google have gone beyond simply paying lip service to that philosophy. They've made it company policy. "At Google, we encourage the spirit of 20 Percent Time," Mayer explains. "Our employees focus 20 percent of their time on what they love to do most, that is, creatively building something. It might not be their core project at work, but it has to be a creative project. We think we hire people who are smart and capable and give them access to a lot of resources and information. Given those resources, they could build anything they dream, and given the information, they know what will be valuable to the company. Smart people usually build smart, compelling things that are useful. Google News was a 20 percent project and Orkut—now the number one social networking site in Brazil and India—also stemmed from a 20 percent project. I just think when you work on something that inspires you, you put in more energy and time, and that shows. This is a license to dream. When people work on their dream, beautiful things happen."

✳ FINDING YOUR EDGE

As you begin to build your marketing plan, ask yourself if you have an edge. If you do, state it in one sentence. How does your product or service solve a problem or fill a need? What obvious and desired benefit does it provide? Does it immediately stir interest, excitement, controversy, or demand? Most of all, in what way is it unique? What quality about it is most likely to gain immediate attention?

If the product or service has no unique or meaningful edge, no amount of marketing is going to make it a success. A survey done through the Eureka Ranch marketing think tank shows that a bad idea is more than twice as often at fault in a business failure than is product performance or the marketing campaign. If consumers aren't drawn to the product or service because it doesn't fulfill a need or desire or it doesn't capture their attention, forget it. No amount of marketing genius is going to help. Be sure that what you're marketing has an edge. As Seth Godin puts it in his book, *Purple Cow*:

> Remarkable marketing is the art of building things worth noticing right into your product or service. Not just slapping on the marketing function as a last-minute add-on, but also understanding from the outset if your offering isn't remarkable, then it's invisible.

On the other hand, a great product or service can fail because consumers don't know about it. The marketing message lacks a unique edge that gets attention and gets people talking. To get a clearer sense of which messages have an edge, think of the ones that have gotten through to you. Which ones did you notice, and why did you notice? What about them made you pay attention, made you laugh, made you want to find out more?

Was it a unique marketing approach? Linda Kaplan Thaler, CEO of The Kaplan Thaler Group, was asked to come up with a campaign for a highly successful, yet little-known insurance company named Aflac. "Here we had a category that has high anxiety and low interest. No one is interested in hearing an insurance commercial." And no one, not even the creatives at her agency, could remember the name until one of them said that by pinching your nose with your fingers and saying the name, it sounded like the call of a duck. They laughed—and they found their edge.

"You need an idea that is both intrusive and disruptive," she explains. "The notion of a duck representing an insurance company that sells insurance for cancer or catastrophic illness or debilitating accidents, this was a disruptive way of thinking. Everyone in the category was doing emotional, dramatic commercials, just-baked oatmeal-cookie advertising, so we felt maybe the real way to reach people was to create reassuring commercials using humor. When we posted our first Aflac commercial in 1999, Aflac received more hits on its Web site in one week than in the entire previous year. The company achieved double-digit growth for four years running."

Linda also was involved in a less disruptive but no less successful campaign for Toys 'R' Us. Like the Aflac campaign, this one required originality. The client wanted a jingle, and Linda was given the responsibility. She waded through a pile of demos from well-known composers but was struggling to find something truly unique.

"I decided that I could only compose this on a children's piano, so I started playing a child's toy piano. That's how I composed it. I wouldn't play it for anyone because it was so childish, and then my creative director heard it and forced me to play it for the client. They tested it against "I Won't Grow Up" from *Peter Pan* and played it for five-year-olds. The kids had never heard of *Peter Pan*, so they didn't know the song. I was sitting in my boss's office [the famous author James Patterson], and he called me and said, 'You now have your first jingle. The five-year-olds love it.'" And the rest was history.

Was it unique publicity? In the 1990s, the Austrian energy drink Red Bull bulled its way into the American market, going toe to toe with the likes of Coke and Pepsi on a much smaller marketing budget, by staging unusual events, such as Flugtag, in which groups and companies build bizarre flying contraptions. The events attracted—and still do—tens of thousands of people and provide Red Bull with significant publicity for free.

Many other campaigns, large and small, have succeeded in the same way—their unique approach, their edge, got people talking. With today's technology, it's easier than ever before to spread the word about your product or service, but you have to have the edge that gets people talking. Your campaign might be smaller and more focused on your local area, but the same rule applies—have an edge.

✳ A STICKY EDGE

The question then becomes, of course, how do you know when you have found your edge? What unique qualities must it possess? In their best-selling and enormously influential book, *Made to Stick*, brothers Chip and Dan Heath use the term *stickiness* to talk about those qualities that will grab attention and hold it.

"A sticky idea is a simple, unexpected, concrete, credible, emotional story," Dan Heath explained to us. "Lots of sticky ideas have only a few of these traits, but some have all six, like John F. Kennedy's famous call to put a man on the moon and return him safely before the end of the decade. It's simple—easy to understand, easy to explain. It's unexpected—in 1961, putting a man on the moon sounded like science fiction. It's amazingly concrete—notice how easy it is to visualize the moment of success, the moment when a human being sets foot on the moon. It was credible because it came from the mouth of a popular president. It's emotional—it appealed to our yearning to reach the next frontier (and, let's not forget, our desire to beat the Soviets). And it's the story of a journey, in miniature."

The question *then* becomes, how do you assess your idea to make sure that it has most or even all of these attributes?

"My brother and I spent years analyzing what makes ideas successful," Heath said. "We studied the full panorama of successful ideas—everything from Aesop's fables to ad campaigns to high school history lessons. And what inspired us to write the book was that we started to spot patterns. We noticed that you could spot a trait, like concreteness, in a successful urban legend—and then spot that same trait at work in a successful public health message. For instance, notice that most urban legends—such as 'You only use 10 percent of brain'—have the same quality of unexpectedness that JFK's man-on-the-moon speech had.

"Ideas draw strength from unexpectedness. Most sticky ideas surprise us or challenge the way we think about the world. Think about the Atkins diet as an example. It spread like wildfire! It was irresistible as an idea because it contradicted everything we thought we knew about diets. Diets were supposed to be about self-deprivation; you're supposed to lose weight by eating small portions of low-fat foods like broccoli and sprouts and carrots. Then the Atkins diet said you lose weight by eating unlimited portions of high-protein, high-fat foods. It was as mind-blowing as a nutritional message can get. Or think about the huge success of the original iMac line of computers, which came in vivid colors and were named after fruit (the Grape iMac). Computers were supposed to be serious and businesslike. They weren't supposed to be bright orange."

Heath points to the need for compromise within organizations as the culprit for the fact that so many ideas are thrust into the marketplace without an edge.

"When five people with very different views need to compromise, where do they meet?" he asks. "In the middle, naturally. But stickiness is at the edge, not in the middle. So when you've got to resolve conflicting opinions, resist the urge to strike a lukewarm compromise. Instead, duke it out, pick one idea, and run with it. Make a decision. Prioritize. There's a certain amount of bravery that's necessary to make an idea stick because it means you're saying something clearly and distinctively, and that's a risk. (What if people think it's stupid? Or impractical? Or wrong?) But it's a risk well worth taking because, in my judgment, there's nothing more powerful than a good idea that sticks."

※ ASSESSING YOUR EDGE

Bryan Eisenberg, author of a best-selling book on marketing entitled *Waiting for Your Cat to Bark?* recalled in a recent interview a friend in Springfield, Missouri, a jeweler, who would replace anyone's watch battery for free, even if the watch wasn't purchased from his store. This might sound like a small gesture, but think of how that gesture would make you feel. You'd be inclined to go to that store the next time you were shopping for jewelry, and you would pass along this tale of generosity.

Eisenberg says that the key to grabbing customers is to be, in a word, *remarkable*.

"You have to offer a remarkable experience that is relevant to them and that makes them want to talk about it," Eisenberg says. "They must share it and be delighted with it, and that leads to customer retention. Remarkable is about what's in the eyes of the customer."

✷ ANALYZE YOUR EDGE

Given the advice we've presented so far in this chapter, step back and look at your idea objectively. Does it have enough of an edge—the right edge, one that's sharp enough to cut through the clutter and reach the people who want what you're selling? Big companies and marketing agencies test the waters with in-depth research, conducting surveys and focus groups to determine if they have an edge and, if so, if it is the *right* edge for the audience they're hoping to reach.

If you're creating a campaign for a small company, or if you're on your own, you probably lack the resources to conduct elaborate research. So begin by testing the edge on the person who matters most—you. Does it engage you? Delight you? Is it unique within the market you want to reach? Sometimes when an idea is new to us or to our companies, we assume that customers also will see it as new. Don't fool yourself. Make sure that your message, product, or service is new to customers—something fresh that will grab their attention.

Next, think about how relevant your edge is to your market. We hear a lot about "brand relevance" these days, and this simply means, do your customers care about what you're offering? Is the edge in your product or service ningful to their lives in some way? Is the edge in your marketing message ne that will inspire them to act? Do you have just a clever gimmick, or does your edge speak to the needs and desires of the people you hope to reach? Will someone buy it when no one is looking, standing there, or encouraging the sale?

Finally, consider how quickly people can understand and process your edge. In short, do they *get* it right away? Paul Hartunian, for example, knew that it took only a second for someone to read, "Man sells Brooklyn Bridge," and get the joke. He also knew instinctively that his plan to literally sell the Brooklyn Bridge would resonate with a large number of people and that the media would embrace it.

If you're still unsure, test your edge on the types of people you want to reach—professional women, perhaps, or teenagers or baby boomers. Give it to them in a sentence, and study their reaction. Do they *get* it? Does it cause an immediate reaction, the one you're hoping to trigger? Is your idea, product, service, or campaign different from what's already available? A "me too" business or marketing plan is not going to attract the level of interest you're hoping to find. Finally, is it relevant to them? Does it speak to a need?

If people's faces light up when they hear your brief description, you probably have the edge that will draw attention, and you're ready to move forward.

If you're not quite getting the response that you want, take time to study what's happening right now—in the news, in society. What are people buzzing about? What people and ideas are capturing the headlines and the spotlight? Then try to figure out why. What edge is capturing everyone's attention, and is there a way of sharpening the edge of your own product, service, or marketing campaign so that you, too, will have your audience buzzing? Remember: It's not easy to create an edge. Sometimes you might happen on a great idea right out of the blue, but in most cases, finding the right edge requires time and patience and trial and error. But if you don't seek it, you'll never find it. Keep trying. Make your message clear and appealing. If you do, people will care. ✳

CHAPTER 4

Think Benefit

Never treat your audience as customers, always as partners.

—James Stewart

Subway restaurants pride themselves on serving sandwiches made with fresh ingredients. They also offer a wide variety of sandwiches so that they can appeal to the tastes of myriad customers. Since the time the company started back in 1965, it has developed a quick-and-easy system that allows customers to order and receive their food quickly.

All these features have helped the company succeed. But what has truly led to the phenomenal growth of the business is that its food is good for you. It's healthy as well as tasty. In the world of fast food, this benefit has made Subway unique—and successful. When we think of fast food, we think of greasy hamburgers and french fries. At Subway, you can eat fast when you're on the go and not feel like you've blown your diet or given yourself heartburn or, worse, the greater likelihood of a heart attack. Eating fast but healthy was a benefit many people could understand and value. Subway had found the core benefit of its product.

To emphasize this core benefit, the company began a promotional campaign in early 2000 featuring a young man named Jared Fogle who had lost more than 200 pounds following what he called the "Subway diet." The marketers at Subway had heard about Jared through an article in *Men's Health* magazine entitled, "Crazy Diets that Work." Although they were concerned about liability issues, Jared was living proof that if the Subway diet may not work for everyone, it certainly worked for him. Within a week, Subway received an avalanche of calls from media outlets including *USA Today*, ABC News, Fox

News, and *Oprah*. Sales at Subway soared. Jared Fogle continues to be the face of Subway and has developed a successful career as a motivational speaker.

✳ WHAT'S IN IT FOR ME?

As you develop your idea, put yourself in your customer's place. Ask yourself, how does my product or service benefit the customer? How does it make customers' lives better or easier or more fulfilling?

As we said earlier, when you deliver your marketing message, customers want to know what's in it for them. They don't care how you came up with the idea or about the specific technology behind how the idea works or what innovative strategies you used in developing the idea. They want to know in clear, specific terms how they benefit by buying what you have to sell. How does it solve a problem they face? They have more purchase options than ever before in the history of humankind. They have more avenues to make those purchases too. An idea that doesn't isolate a real need within a market and provide a meaningful response to that need will remain invisible.

You must fill a need—the bigger, the better. You must solve a problem—the bigger, the better. You must provide something completely new that consumers do not even realize they need but will understand and appreciate and, ultimately, desire.

✳ SIZZLE ALONE WILL FIZZLE

The famous cliché in marketing that tells us that "it's not the steak, it's the sizzle" has been misinterpreted through the years to mean that *only* the sizzle is important. Not true. No amount of sizzle is going to sell a bad steak. Sure, it might attract attention for a while, but repeat business is not going to happen.

Joel Babbit, chief creative officer of Atlanta-based ad agency Grey Worldwide and president of New York–based GCI, one of the world's largest public relations firms, concurs, citing a well-known marketing axiom: the fastest way to kill a bad product is with great advertising.

"This is a famous quote that focuses on the primary dilemma of my business—advertising and public relations," Babbit says. "The job of our industry is to promote brands and to communicate positive information in the hopes that the target market will respond favorably. Responding favorably usually translates to things like making a purchase or visiting a retail location or trying a new product. But what happens when that purchase or that visit or that product creates a negative experience? When that happens, no amount of promotion or communication can improve the situation. In fact, as the quote above illustrates, the better the advertising, the faster people will respond, and if their experience is negative, that good advertising will only quicken the brand's demise.

"Therefore, it is critical to analyze the customer experience being offered and to ensure that it is a positive and meaningful one before any promotional dollars are spent.

"The best example of this is the success of Target. There have always been a number of competitors for this 'big box' mass merchandiser, and many of them spend huge amounts of dollars on advertising and promotion. For years, these competitors were at parity in the type of merchandise offered, the level of service provided, and their pricing. Yet their advertising sought vainly to communicate how different they were from one another.

"Finally, Target stepped back to look not at their promotion, but at their product. They began to make real, concrete changes. They engaged a number of high-fashion designers to develop new merchandise lines. They added more innovative product categories. They renovated their stores to be hip and modern. Only then did they introduce a new advertising campaign that reflected the changes made. The other competitors continued with their massive advertising spending but without any meaningful changes to their offering. The bottom line is this: Success cannot start with the promotional phase. It must start far earlier in the development of what is being offered."

✳ BIG SOLUTION, BIG SALES

How does your idea solve a problem in a *significantly* better, faster, and/or cheaper way than the competition? Your benefit must be one that customers can perceive quickly. If your idea is only slightly better than the competition, customers may not even recognize it at all, or if they do, they may not recognize it as particularly valuable to them.

In his book, *Free Prize Inside*, well-known author Seth Godin cites the example of a marketing campaign by Continental Airlines that focused on the fact that the company's planes were the newest in the market. In fact, they were only a few months younger than those of several key competitors. "Being somewhere near an edge," Godin writes, "is a thing marketers do when they think people care enough to really dig deeply. But since they don't, you don't win by going near an edge. You win by going all the way to the limit of the edge and overwhelming it."

As we discussed earlier, you need to have an edge, and your edge must contain a benefit that leaves the competition in the dust. It must stand out, and it must be one that your target market needs—that possesses an intrinsic value in their lives.

Give yourself this test: When you think about your idea, what quality gives you the greatest sense of pride? Who are you helping? How are you helping them? If you're entering the marketing fray with a "me too" proposition, it's not going to excite you, and it's not going to excite anyone else. If you're not yet feeling that sense of pride that comes from delivering something that makes a meaningful difference in the lives of others, you're not ready yet. Keep working your idea until you feel that pride and passion about it.

✳ COURTING SUCCESS

Alex Carroll was a courier driver in college. Like most courier drivers, he collected a few speeding tickets along the way. Ten, to be exact. With a few suggestions from of a couple of his cop buddies, he managed to beat eight of his ten tickets and keep his license and courier job. Figuring that a lot of people would be interested in avoiding costly fines, he decided to write and self-publish a little book of all the tricks he'd learned on how to beat speeding tickets. He entitled it, *Beat the Cops: The Guide to Fighting Your Traffic Ticket and Winning*.

Lacking money for a promotion budget, he got the word out by doing radio interviews—more than 1,200! He obviously had a message that producers knew would interest their audiences. The interviews didn't cost Carroll anything, and he could do them from home by telephone. He ended up selling over a quarter of a million books and generating millions in sales. He now has a training course and resource package that helps others get on radio shows and promote whatever they have to promote. By thinking creatively, offering a solution, and filling a need, he built a new career for himself.

✳ BIG MARKET, NOT NECESSARILY BIG SALES

Too often marketers focus on the size of the market rather than on the size of the problem that's being solved. Attempts by a variety of industries—especially book publishers—to grab the huge market of NASCAR fans have failed because the products they offered didn't provide a needed benefit for those customers. In developing the idea, these industries were blinded by the dollar signs implicit in the sheer number of people in the market. They failed to think like the customer and deliver a real value to those customers.

A well-known example of this type of thinking occurred in the early 1990s when Coca-Cola went after the Gen X and Gen Y markets with a new product called OK Soda. The product design and the anti-advertising advertising tried to appeal to the cynicism of the disaffected (but mushrooming) grunge market. The message: "Hey, kids, it's OK to feel that life sucks, and with OK Soda you'll feel like it really doesn't suck as much as you thought." The test marketing proved disastrous. The kids already felt like it was OK and didn't need a major corporation to tell them so. And therefore, despite a huge market, brilliant package design, and innovative marketing, the product failed because it didn't supply a needed benefit.

Years ago, a popular FM radio station created a mock company called "Brute Force Cybernetics" that "produced" absurd and hilarious products that served no recognizable function whatsoever. The company's slogan was "Creating a need—and then filling it." The series of commercials satirized the practice among marketers to create the perception of a need in order to justify the existence of their products.

When you think about benefit to the customer, you will ensure your idea has a purpose and therefore a market.

✳ IT'S ONLY A MOVIE

Reed Hastings was the CEO of a small software company back in the mid-1990s when he returned a movie he'd rented. As he recalled on *60 Minutes*, "I'd rented a VHS, and I had misplaced it, and it was six weeks late. So it was a 40-dollar late fee. I remember because I didn't want to tell my wife. . . . And I thought, 'Oh, great! Now I'm thinking about lying to my wife about a late fee and the sanctity of my marriage for this thing!' I mean it was just crazy. And I was on the way to the gym, and I realized—'Whoa! Video stores could operate like a gym, with a flat membership fee.' And it was like 'I wonder why no one's done that before!'"

Haven't most of us been in a similar circumstance—the movie that goes missing, and suddenly we're faced with paying a high late fee. Video stores, Hastings knew, were forced to charge the fees because they had limited supplies. When a movie isn't available, they lose the rental fee. As an experienced software engineer, he found a way to create an online network that would earn its money from membership fees rather than from the rentals themselves, offering its members a significant benefit: keep the movie as long as you want, and avoid late fees.

The benefit-driven idea for his new company—Netflix—was born.

But he didn't stop there. He also knew from personal experience that video store customers often are frustrated by making a trip to the store only to find that the movie they want isn't available. All the copies have been rented, or the store doesn't carry the title. But a virtual store based on a computer network would not be limited by the space of a bricks-and-mortar store. It could offer tens of thousands of movies.

Timing, however, was a crucial part of his idea. Without an actual store, Netflix would mail the movies to its customers. At that time, DVD technology was beginning to replace VHS, which was fortunate for Hastings. A VHS cartridge could be damaged en route. Would a DVD survive the journey?

"I ran down to Tower [Records] and bought a bunch and mailed them to myself, and then I waited," Hastings recalled on *60 Minutes*. "I opened them up. And they were fine. And I thought, 'Oh my God. This is going to work! This is going to work!'"

And he was right. By offering new and meaningful benefits that customers valued—and ones Hastings himself valued—Netflix earned $688 million in revenues in 2006.

✳ PIZZA IS PIZZA

Trying to be everything to everyone is a recipe for failure. If you believe that your product or service targets "everyone," you don't yet know your customer or have a clear sense of direction. What you offer has to be something that a certain market finds valuable—even indispensable. And what one market wants another doesn't want. By trying to reach all markets, you risk missing them all.

Case in point: Domino's pizza. Domino's delivers quality pizza, but does it offer a wide range of exotic toppings and all sorts of crusts the way some of the other places do? Well, no. And yet, since its founding in 1960 by two

Michigan brothers (one of the brothers traded his share of the business a year later for a Volkswagon beetle), it has grown into the second-largest pizza chain in the world, opening its eight-thousandth franchise in 2006.

The key to this extraordinary success in a competitive and look-alike field is that Domino's delivers inexpensive but reliably average pizza fast. For many customers, pizza is pizza. They don't see the value in a wide selection of fresh toppings or in extra spices or some type of exotic crust. They want it quickly, and they don't want to pay a lot for it. They don't want bad pizza, of course, but mediocre is okay as long as it's the same level of mediocrity every time. The lesson for Domino's success is that not only does it have to provide a benefit, but it also has to provide one to customers who value it. No doubt dozens of pizza chains offering tastier pizza than Domino's have come and gone during the time that Domino's has continued its climb toward the top of the industry. Some that targeted the lower-price market have faded away during that time too for presenting themselves *only* as a commodity rather than as consistent, no-frills quality for less money. Domino's succeeded by targeting its customer with real and valued benefits and presenting its message clearly and often.

For some time, as you might recall, Domino's even offered a 30-minute guarantee. Customers who waited longer than 30 minutes for their pizza to arrive were given a free pizza. When the delivery staff began showing up in a number of traffic accidents, this program was discontinued, but it did cement in the minds of customers that Domino's was committed to getting a pizza to them faster than anyone else. The campaign centered on a ringing doorbell followed by the line, "Get the door, it's Domino's," and it emphasizes the benefits of speed and reliability rather than taste. It may not be the world's best pizza, but it's here!

Successful businesses target specific needs with what they offer. They don't try to be everything to everyone. They provide benefits that serve real needs and provide real solutions to a specific market of customers.

To create such an idea, you have to know your customer, which is the subject we'll cover in the next chapter. As you're no doubt already beginning to see, the *Wow* success system is based on layers. Each of the laws is related to the other laws, and as you more clearly understand—and use—this system, you have a greater chance of achieving your *Wow* success.

✳ FOLLOW THE BOUNCING BALL

Sometimes your idea is so inventive that it fills a need or provides a solution in ways that surprise and delight—that create their own need. Michele Kapustka realized this fact when she created SENDaBALL.com. Based in Chicago, she started sending balls in 1996 to family and friends, and sales have been rolling upward ever since. One of the first balls she sent was "Have a ball with your new baby." She sent the message on a 10-inch play ball, the kind you can find at a drug or dime store in the bins, ready to bounce. Michele, a former creative director for a direct-mail company, figured out how to stamp the ball and send it through the mail free of a box or wrapping.

The response was so overwhelming that Michele did it again and again. A few years later, while standing in line at the post office with an armful of balls, she was approached by a gentleman who inquired about the balls. He asked if she was in the business of sending them and wondered if she could send a ball to a friend of his who was ill. She told him how he could send one, but as the line progressed, she agreed to mail a ball for him for $5.00. As she left the post office, she called her sister, Melissa, and told her that someone hired her to send a ball. Her sister began screaming, and by early evening, the two of them had designed a Web site and were open for business.

Inspired by an episode of *Oprah* featuring women who started their own businesses with their own unique ideas, Michele and Melissa were ready to give their greeting balls a shot. Now, for $19.99, these entrepreneurial sisters will send a ball through the mail with a variety of what they call "pun-tastic sayings" such as "Bounce back soon!" and "Have a ball on your birthday!" To date, SENDaBALL has sold over 50,000 personalized balls.

Was there a crying need among consumers to send balls through the mail instead of greeting cards? Well, no. But are people always looking for creative gifts for friends and family—a gift or greeting with a little something extra that will brighten a day and be remembered years later? You betcha. ✳

CHAPTER 5

Know Your Customer

In business, you get what you want by giving other people what they want.

—Alice MacDougall

I t's 1951 in Mt. Vernon, New York. Seated at a yellow Formica table in her kitchen, paging through women's magazines, a young woman spends hours studying the ads. She is trying to figure out who the ads are trying to reach. Who are the customers for these products? She finally reaches some conclusions and decides to start small with just two products. She places an ad in *Seventeen* magazine offering a monogrammed handbag and a matching belt. To her delight, she receives 50 orders. From those first sales she builds a catalogue business that now reaches 21 million people. Her name is Lillian Vernon.

She recalled the story in an article for SCORE, Counselors to America's Small Business, entitled, "Make Someone Happy—Your Customer."

"I didn't realize it then, but everything I ever needed to know about selling I was learning at my kitchen table," she writes. "I was learning how to identify, find, and keep customers."

Vernon developed a system of index cards, on which she wrote details about the customers—the products they ordered and their tastes. Although the company's outstanding growth made the index cards obsolete, the principle continues to form the foundation of the company's philosophy, which is based on trust. "Trust is established when people—or a company and its customers—understand and rely on each other," Vernon writes.

To create and sustain such a relationship with your customers, you have to know who they are. You have to understand their needs and their tastes. As you develop your *Wow*, keep in mind what your customers want. There is no point in having a *Wow* if you don't know who needs it.

 ## KYC

The acronym *KYC*–"Know your customer"–is used in the financial world to describe the due diligence that is done before an investment or sale is made. But we're using it to address one of the key laws of *Wow* success. It resonates through nearly every other law in our system. You can't "think benefit" if you don't know who you're benefiting. You can't create or sharpen your edge if you don't know who you want to reach.

One of the fundamental principles in the work of best-selling author and speaker on the subject of business leadership Marcus Buckingham is a simple question: "Who do you serve?" Without an answer to this question, he posits, you're going to struggle for success, and you won't be able to be a true leader. Without an answer to this question, you won't be able to give your "followers" a clear understanding of your goals. You need to know who you are seeking to please, whose needs you are trying to fill. Buckingham speaks to leading companies, and he often asks this question. To him, it is so basic to a company's business that it goes without saying, but he often finds that his audience doesn't have a clear answer. In an interview for Toastmasters, Buckingham recalled a presentation he made for a huge financial institution:

> I asked, "Who do you serve?" And they said, "People with more than $500,000 in investable assets." That's a terrible answer. As a follower, I still don't know, who is this guy? What does he need from us?

"This guy," of course, is the customer. And if you or the people who work for you don't know that customer well, can't envision his or her needs, desires, and traits, then you'll have a tough time isolating the right benefit and cutting through the noise of marketing messages with one that has a sharply honed edge.

✳ LOST AT SEA

"If you don't know what you're fishing for, how will you know what size boat to bring?" asks David L. Sack, director of wealth management at Smith Barney, who has achieved great success in the investment arena. He explains that early in his career he worked hard and achieved a level of success but lacked a guiding vision of his market.

"Because I hadn't found my target market, I was swinging all over the place, constantly changing. I used a shotgun approach rather than a rifle approach." After several years in sales, Sack moved to a management position, but after a few more years, he wanted to return to sales. This time, however, he developed a guiding vision first.

His ideal client would be the owner of a privately held manufacturing company with more than one family member in the business. He or she would be based within a hundred-mile radius of New York City and have a minimum of $500,000 in a retirement plan.

As Sack explained, the owner of a business is a decision maker and a risk taker, especially in a manufacturing company, which requires significant capital investment from the start. As for family involvement, Sack says that it takes more than one generation to build true wealth, and a parent is not going to invite a son or daughter into a business that isn't working or isn't worthwhile. With these guidelines in mind, he knew quite a bit about his prospects and his customers.

Sack recalls a time when this knowledge of the customer paid off particularly well. He received a call on a Friday about a man "with a lot of money looking for someone to help with investing," he says. From what he'd been told, the man fit Sack's criteria as a potential client. "I thought, if this person is real, he's going to want to test me," he says. He figured that the owner of a successful manufacturing company valued hard work and was looking for commitment and dedication from the people he hired. "I thought, 'I'll bet you he calls me tonight,'" Sacks says. "So even though it was a Friday evening, I hung around. At ten after seven, he called. That's how I landed the business. I anticipated [that] if the person was for real and he got a voice mail saying gone for the evening, he may have taken his business elsewhere."

✳ BE INTERESTED VERSUS INTERESTING

Pat Burns, a popular speaker and accomplished entrepreneur and the author of *Grandparent Rocks*, shared with us a poignant story. "My former business partner and mentor, Marshall Thurber, an author, attorney, and inventor, taught me many lessons, but one has influenced me for my entire career. He taught me [that] in business and in life and when you're speaking, 'stop trying to be interesting and instead be interested.' He taught me the gift of being interested, and that's always stuck with me. When I think about people who have this ability, I think about Ken Blanchard and Art Linkletter. When they got on stage, you can hear a pin drop. They are fun to listen to and are simply so captivating. Their secret? They are just being real. The minute we focus on 'I'm the best at this or that,' we lose our ability to connect. It all boils down to you and your customer—or you and me. The question to ask yourself is, 'Do we like each other?' Liking each other and being interested in each other is what matters most."

✳ DESIGNER GALS

Jeanne Fitzmaurice's brainchild has created hundreds of thousands of gals—virtual ones, that is. Her "Design-her Gals" are twenty-first century paper-like dolls you create online who live in an interactive site called Designhergals.com. It was a stroke of genius and good timing in 2005 that enabled Jeanne to capitalize on the personal avatar market in a totally unique way. Her *Wow* was developing proprietary technology that allows users to create their virtual likeness by selecting from hundreds of hairstyle, skin tone, eye color, outfit and accessory options, and then creating one of a kind stationery and gift items for themselves or their friends. Jeanne's stylish gals hit it big and are currently embraced by over 250,000 community members, high profile celebrities, and corporations around the world. What makes this site so irresistible? Not only does Design-her Gals provide a creative outlet for its users where they can design a look-alike caricature of themselves or another gal pal, but it also produces totally unique gifts that are personalized. It also sheds light on an important topic in a whimsical way by raising funds for stage IV breast cancer patients and their families through its nonprofit Gal to Gal Foundation.

※ THE CUSTOMER CONNECTION

As you develop your brand, your marketing campaign, and your product or service, you should have one person in the center of your mind—your customer. The reason is simple. When your customers are considering a purchase, whose needs are they thinking about? The question, of course, is rhetorical, but let's go ahead and say it for the record—their own! When you are developing your *Wow* idea, you should have that customer's needs in mind too. By taking this approach, you're already sharing a common goal with the customer, and this is the first step toward reaching that customer.

This idea seems pretty basic, but far too often new businesses don't give it enough thought. You may have been tempted to skip this chapter yourself, feeling that you already know your customer. You may even have a few charts and graphs to prove it. Before moving on, however, give yourself this test. Ask yourself

- What is my business?
- What is my job?
- What is my brand?

Each of your answers should involve your customer directly. Each answer should be, shall we say, customercentric. For example, let's say that a graphic designer who has started her own business to sell a fun new line of greeting cards is asking the questions. She responds, "I run a small business that produces and sells innovative, high-quality specialty cards and stationery with unique messages for the gift market. My job is to create the messages, design the cards, and oversee their production. My brand focuses on a stylized design and upscale look printed on high-quality paper. There's nothing quite like it in the marketplace today."

Our designer sits back and beams a confident smile, feeling sure that we're impressed.

We're not.

Her answers focus on the product, its features, and her day-to-day duties but make no mention of her customers. If we asked her to speak specifically about her customers, she probably could come up with a response, but the main point of this law is that your customers should be part of everything you do and every decision you make. The first question to ask yourself is the one Marcus Buckingham asked his audience: "Who do you serve?"

No feature you offer has value unless it's one that a clearly visualized customer group finds valuable. No amount of clever marketing is going to succeed unless you know what your customers want and how your product or service satisfies that desire. You need to know how your customers think and talk about the need, where your customers will hear about you, and how much money those customers will pay.

A better answer from our card designer might be: "I create messages on beautiful cards that give young, middle-class women between the ages of 16 and 30 a means to articulate their thoughts and feelings to the people in their lives—family, friends, and coworkers—in an honest, sometimes funny way that more accurately reflects their true selves and manner of speech than cards they can find at traditional gift stores."

When you know the true needs and desires of your customers, you're on your way to reaching them.

As *USA Today* small-business columnist Rhonda Adams writes:

> Although we think we know our customers well, the reality is we probably don't. Most of us, after all, develop our products or services because we ourselves recognize a need in the market. I know dozens of entrepreneurs who started their businesses because there was something they wanted to buy that just didn't exist. As a result, many of our products or services tend to reflect our own interests, needs, and abilities. Those aren't necessarily the interests or needs of our target customers. In our rush to get a product out the door or to get our company up and running, we don't have the time—or money—to do a lot of market research.

YOU ARE NOT YOUR CUSTOMER

One of the most common mistakes in marketing is focusing on yourself and your product or service. An important point many marketers and business owners forget is that they are not "the customer." You might fit your customer profile, and if you weren't offering the product or service, you might be someone who would purchase it, but as soon as you put on your marketing hat, you have joined the other team. Your main desire shifted from wanting something to selling that something. There's a difference—one you should always keep in mind.

It's helpful, of course, to be part of the group to whom you're selling because you can trust your instincts better and probably will have easier access to others in that group. Just remember that you're not the market. The customers you're seeking don't live and breathe your product or service the way you do. They're far less keenly aware of it, which means that they're far less able to notice subtle differences between you and your competitors. They have many other choices and are being bombarded with many other messages about other products and services. They have their own lives and jobs and families to think about. They don't care about the business you're in. They care about their own needs and desires. It's your job to convince them that you can fulfill those needs and desires.

To get a better understanding of this concept, consider the two primary questions you must answer to begin knowing your customers:

1. Who has the greatest need for your product or service?
2. Who has the greatest willingness to pay for it?

Now ask yourself

1. Do I need my product or service?
2. Am I you willing to pay for it?

Of course, you don't need your own product or service. You already possess it.

And since you already possess it, you aren't willing to pay for it. Keep this little quiz handy, and use it the next time you trick yourself into thinking that you're the customer. It's an easy trap to fall into and one that has gobbled up many an enterprising business owner.

✳ KNOWING YOUR CUSTOMER

Big businesses spend millions of dollars on qualitative and quantitative research. They commission focus groups and run surveys. They hire researchers to do point-of-purchase and even home interviews to find out what customers are thinking. And this costly research can be money well spent. If you have millions of dollars and a crack team of researchers at your disposal, by all means use them. If not, there are other ways to get to know your customer.

First, try to meet as many of your customers as possible in person. Talk to them, and don't limit the conversation to your product or service. Find out what else they buy and what they do in their lives. Find out about their hopes and dreams and passions and fears. During these conversations, look for patterns of need and behavior. Ask the same question in different ways, and listen for changes in response.

Another great source of information about your customers is the Internet. In recent years, some marketers have cursed the Internet because it has produced such an explosion of advertising messages through which they must find a way to cut. But the Internet also has made market research easier than ever before. People everywhere are writing their opinions in blogs, forums, and chat groups. We may not always like what we hear, but we certainly can hear it! Use the technology to speak directly to your customers and create an open environment that embraces candor and welcomes honesty, even if the message is negative.

Read the trade magazines and Web sites in your field. Keep up with trends. Find out which businesses are doing well, which aren't, and why. Again, though, don't limit your research to the trade journals. Remember, like you, those folks are in the business. They're not the customer. Expand your reading to include the publications and Web sites that your customers are reading—and often participating in through blogs and forums. If you've come up with a new type of tent that is easy to carry and easier to set up, for example, don't limit your research to the outdoor-recreation industry journals. Read *Backpacker* and *Camping Life*. Read them through the eyes of your customers. Find out if your tent-camper prefers to fish or paddle a kayak. Find out if his or her biggest need is to teach his or her children about safe hiking practices or to protect the environment.

"The single most important lesson I've learned in my career is to put yourself in the place of your audience," say Stephen Burgay, a marketing essional and brand manager for many years with John Hancock Life surance and now at Boston University. "Think about your product, its features, and how you sell it, through the eyes of your consumer. You have to put it in terms they can relate to, that they see as valuable to them."

Burgay says he sees too many marketing programs that focus on the corporation and how great it is rather than on the customers' needs. "It's all about the corporation," he says. "Those campaigns fail to connect with consumers. The consumer wants to know what it can do for me. Good marketing starts with the proposition of how this product benefits you. You have to think and see and talk like a consumer."

✸ JUST ASK

In 1994, Susan Packard helped to start a new cable television network, HGTV, that has developed into one of the most successful brands in cable television history, with millions of loyal viewers. She says that a key component of that success was creating avenues for customer feedback.

"Our key founder had a good idea—a cable channel dedicated to all things around the home," she recalls. "There was no dedicated cable network on the subject, and that was the key idea. We then made it a very big idea by grouping other things around it. That included commerce, a Web site, a call center, a membership club, a magazine. Through the call center, we were able to talk to our viewers directly. The phone number was shown on air after each show, and viewers used it. We completed the loop for them by answering their questions. We gave them involvement in the brand. Over time, we've taken that online. But they still find us to ask us their questions, and we are responsive to them." She and her colleagues have taken the same approach to invent new cable channels, such as The Food Network.

Packard also notes that a business often has more than one customer base. "We have three customers in cable TV," she explains. "We have the viewer, the advertisers, and the cable operator or satellite provider. It's a three-legged stool. The brands that I've worked on were understanding and respectful of all three sets of customers. You have to understand who your customers are."

✳ CREATING YOUR CUSTOMER

It's become more and more common at marketing agencies to create a fictional customer who personifies the person the agency wants to reach. The marketers mix together a stew of demographic, geographic, personality, and behavioral information and cook up a single person who has a name, a hometown, and the various specific qualities of the target market. By naming this fictional customer, the agency can relate to him or her more easily. It's tough to create meaningful messages and stir brand loyalty when your audience is a bunch of slices in a pie chart or percentages in a marketing report.

Whether or not you decide to name your ideal customer is up to you, but take the time to know as much as possible about the real person buying what you have to sell. Ask yourself the five journalistic questions, and spare no time or effort on your answers:

1. *Who is my customer?* Determine as many aspects of the person as possible—age, gender, income level, marital and family situation, and areas of interests. Am I seeking business customers or individuals?

2. *What need do I fill for my customer?* Explore your customer's personality and behavior—what frustrations are you resolving? What hopes are you helping your customer to realize? What fears are you quelling? What lifestyle are you helping your customer to live? What aspects of self-image are you catering to?

3. *Where is my customer?* Can you reach your target market with your message? Where does your customer find out information (the newspaper, radio, television, Web sites, organizations, meetings, etc.)? Can you make it available in the places where your customer will find it and buy it?

When will I be able to reach my customer? In today's faster-paced world, timing is crucial, as we'll discuss later in this book, but spend time on this question. Are you on the cutting edge of a trend, or will your customer's need be filled before you can reach him or her? Also ask yourself when your customer is most likely to buy. Is your product or service seasonal? Is the customer's need felt more keenly at certain times of the day, week, or year?

5) *How does your customer feel about the need you're fulfilling?* Is it important? Will he or she be skeptical? Will he or she recognize how your product or service is valuable?

Before launching your brand or marketing campaign, know the answers to these questions. When someone asks you who will want what you have to sell, your answer should *not* be, "Everyone will want it." This is a clear indication that you don't yet know your customer. Many businesses like to crow about "customer service," but not enough take the time to truly know who they're serving. And if you don't know, how will you anticipate that customer's needs and concerns and that customer's frustrations and objections, the little things that will make the experience for the customer memorable and satisfying.

Orvel Ray Wilson, president of the Guerilla Group marketing firm, puts it simply: "Customers buy for their reasons, not yours." When you know the reasons they buy, you've truly got something to sell. ✳

PART 2

Outstanding, Outrageous,
and Out of the Box

CHAPTER 6

Keep It Simple

Simplicity is the ultimate sophistication.

—**Leonardo da Vinci**

he elevator doors open, and you step aboard, nodding to the person who is already there. As the elevator ascends, you both agree that the weather has been warm. Then the person asks, "So what business are you in?"

The elevator continues to climb, each floor's number lighting up one by one. You have only 30 seconds or so to explain your fabulous idea before you reach the person's floor. Can you do it? Can you summarize your idea, how it works, and how it delivers an important benefit and to whom it delivers that benefit? If you've prepared what publicists call an "elevator speech," the answer is yes.

Your elevator speech distills your idea, your message, your benefit, your target market, and your plan to its very essence. Impossible? No. In fact, it's essential. The key is keeping everything simple. If your audience is too varied, the idea too complex, or the plan too complicated, you're not going to succeed.

If your response to the tale of the elevator speech is that your idea is just too complicated to explain in 30 seconds, take a step back. Is the problem with the logistics of communicating quickly, or is there a deeper source of trouble? Too often we see marketers focusing on–and struggling with–their "pitch" when the real problem is that the idea isn't fully developed in a clear, simple way. They feel that they've got a great idea, but when they begin writing copy for the brand-new Web site or marketing brochure, they run on for pages and pages, looking for words and images that express the essence of their idea. If you find yourself in a similar predicament, don't focus on the message, twisting it in vain like a Rubik's Cube. Go back and polish the idea into its most basic and brilliant form. As a good news reporter knows, if you are looking to connect with your audience, never bury the lead!

✳ WHO CARES?

As you're developing your idea, ask yourself a simple question: Who cares? The answer, of course, is that you care. The sad corollary to your answer is that when you're starting out, *only* you care. Your job in finding your way to *Wow* success is making other people care, inspiring them to buy what you have to sell and to help you sell it by spreading the word.

As you're formulating your plan, keep it as simple as possible so that your customers understand its relevance and value to them. Remember that all these people—potential customers as well as potential ambassadors for your idea—are busy with their own lives. You have to be able to communicate what you want. You have to make them care by making your message one that applies to them in a way they can't resist. They must have what you're offering. And they must tell others about it.

✳ THINK BIG

Actor Richard Kiel has appeared on the big screen for more than 40 years and is best known for his role of "Jaws" in the James Bond films *The Spy Who Loved Me* and *Moonraker*. From *The Longest Yard* to *Happy Gilmore* to appearances on *The Twilight Zone* and even *The Monkees*, Richard Kiel is instantly recognized across the globe as a consummate actor.

And a big one. At 7 feet, 2 inches tall, with a shoe size of 18 quadruple E, his bigger-than-life, towering appearance might be why some people say that he's a *Wow*, but we think that it has more to do with his tenacity, perseverance, and nonstop positive attitude. While Kiel was growing up, his 5-foot, 9-inch father's favorite saying was, "The harder I work, the luckier I get." His mom, who is 5 feet, 4 inches tall, added, "If wishes were horses, beggars would ride." Richard explains, "My parents taught me [that] you can't wish your way to success or have the things you want in life by hoping things will happen. You have to work for . . . [them]." This gave Kiel a nonstop drive in life to prove himself. With a background in sales, he also knew that you have to be succinct, market yourself, and keep it simple.

Keeping it simple has paid many dividends in Kiel's career. To start, he focused on his unique edge. "My size got me interest, but if I was going to play more than monsters in a rubber suit and dumb-guy roles, I had to get people to know [that] I could do other things. I figured that I couldn't depend on just acting, so I got a compatible job. Selling cars and real estate, I was able to also manage an acting role at the same time. After the role was over, I'd run an ad in *Hollywood Reporter* and *Variety* showing what I did. I spread the word, and that started making better roles happen. I managed to break out of being in a rubber suit.

"*The Longest Yard* was the turning point in my career. Because I hadn't even played college football and they really wanted professional players, I couldn't get an interview. One of my agents got me an appointment with the producer, and I was hired. The director, Robert Aldrich, appreciated my extemporaneous acting skills and encouraged . . . [me]. He loved what I was doing and gave me support. He said, 'Just do more of what you're doing, have fun, and enjoy it.' He appreciated my sense of humor, and he also listened to me, which made me feel really great."

Today, Kiel gets around more quickly in a motorized scooter owing to the challenges that arise from balancing at over 7 feet tall. Because he used a walking stick, his body leaned to one side. His leg muscles tired easily, and he had to prevent falling. The motorized scooter gives him increased mobility, but even with physical difficulties, Kiel views his height as the opportunity that gave him the time to devote to putting other ideas into motion.

Kiel still travels the world with his wife Diane and lets nothing get in his way. He has written screen plays and now has turned his sights to book writing, penning a book entitled, *How to Sell Your House 100 Times as Fast: And Save 60% to 90% in Sales Costs*. Experience continues to be his teacher. Finding a smarter way to do something is his motivation. When he was trying to sell his house, Kiel went from listing it unsuccessfully to making it happen proactively. Kiel summed up his ideas and titled his book to make his point. For Kiel, the word *fast* was not good enough. It had to be larger than life—"100 times faster" makes his point. It's no surprise that Richard Kiel thinks big. Really big. Today, Kiel works hard to accomplish things 100 times faster and continues to make it big. We say 100 times *Wow*!

✳ YADA YADA YADA

In today's enormously fast-paced world, where consumers are processing thousands of messages every day, your message needs to be simple, clear, and direct in order to get through. Listeners have to "get it" immediately—why they need it, how it provides a solution or a service or entertainment or whatever it is you're offering.

To keep it simple, leave out the subtleties—for now. Let the core idea stand on its own. If it can't—if you must take time to explain your idea in detail in order for your target market to understand why they must have it—you've lost your market. This is true whether you're selling a screenplay or a cleanser or an investment plan.

To help you express your idea simply, lead with the primary benefit. If your cleanser makes cleanup for moms easier than ever before, focus on that benefit. Extrapolate it by showing how her life will be more relaxed, and note that she'll have more enjoyable time with the kids because she'll spend less time cleaning their messes. After you've stated the big benefit and the audience clearly understands it, then you can add more information to the mix. If your new cleanser also can be used to freshen the kitty box, for example, leave out that fact until you have your listener hooked. If it's based on a revolutionary chemical reaction developed at NASA, there is no need to mention this right away (unless you know that mom is also a wannabe astronaut).

Another strategy for simplifying your message—and your entire marketing campaign—is to recall ones that attracted you as a customer. What qualities did those messages possess? Why were the messages important and relevant to you? What made them stand out?

✳ SIMPLIFY YOUR BENEFIT

As we discussed in Chapter 4, a key to your success is providing a benefit. You have to have something people want—the solution to a problem, a more efficient system that saves time, or a service that saves people money. In short, you have to "build a better mousetrap." But you have to be able to state that benefit quickly and clearly in such a way that customers immediately recognize its value. Sure, your mousetrap is made with a special aluminum alloy that makes it snap faster and catch more mice, but skip the explanation of the alloy. Sure, you include a bag of cheese squares already cut in a specially designed size that makes them easy to mount in the trap, but leave that discussion out of your pitch. Your customers don't care. They just want rodent-free homes. When you're working on your "elevator speech," keep the benefit to the listener uppermost in your mind. Let it guide you. Hear the speech through the listener's ears.

There's a saying in the business world that continues to be true: "Do one thing well." If you truly have created a better mousetrap, let that be your focus. Seek an audience that needs to be rid of mice. Prove to them through specific examples that their lives will be more enjoyable because your mousetrap has eliminated their problem. Trying to be all things to all people can leave you with no people at all.

☀ SIMPLIFY YOUR MARKET

A well-known example of this approach is that of Wal-Mart. The company's business model was based on providing a wide selection of affordably priced consumer goods to small-town America, which the other "big box" stores did not see as a worthwhile place to put a store. Wal-Mart found and targeted an underserved market and benefited from a lack of competition from stores with far deeper pockets. Slowly, the company expanded into more and more markets and, through its success in these markets, accrued the resources to move into bigger markets. If the company had started by setting up stores in large markets that already had stores offering similar selection and price, who knows what might have happened?

☀ SIMPLIFY YOUR MARKETING PLAN

As you work your way along the road to *Wow* success, keep your eyes focused on your destination, and take the simplest, most direct route. Unless you have a large staff of workers ready to launch your plan with you, we suggest that you make a simple plan and create goals that allow you to measure your success.

To simplify your plan, create clear and simple goals. What do you want to accomplish, and how soon do you want to accomplish it? From that point, work backward, outlining the simplest steps on the way from where you are now to where you want to be. As much as possible, keep the elements in your plan under your control. By this, we mean don't rely on forces beyond your reach. In any market segment, there are trends and situations that could help or undermine you, and it's usually difficult to foresee all of them. Our point is that you shouldn't rely on them in order to succeed. Your plan needs to be anchored in realistic expectations based on circumstances that you can create and control.

As you develop your plan, rely on the contributions of people who you *know* will deliver what you need from them. Be realistic about the time and money you can put into the plan. Hoping for a generous benefactor to pour dollars into your campaign could lead to disappointment down the road. Your cousin's friend may not be quite the software expert you need. Oprah may not pick you as a guest on her show. An apparent market trend may fizzle before you get your product up and running.

✳ A BRUSH WITH DESTINY

Eighty-three-year-old Sam Garrett calls himself a professional salesman. He has been selling since childhood and has sold everything from pantyhose to women's makeup. And yet, women all over the world are indebted to Sam not for his salesmanship but for his creativity: he invented the makeup blusher brush.

In 1959, a friend gave Garrett a little brush to clean the lens on his camera. Garrett realized that a similar brush would help women to apply blush and powder better than the powder puffs he was selling at the time to drug stores. It occurred to Garrett that a painter would never paint a picture with a powder puff, so why would a woman use one to apply her makeup? It was so obvious, so simple that it's amazing that no one had made the connection before. Garrett showed his brush to a friend who worked at Saks Fifth Avenue in Palo Alto, California, and asked her to use it to find out if she liked it better than the powder puff. She said that it worked better because women could put the makeup just where they wanted it to go. On the strength of that endorsement, Garrett mailed $180 to a friend in Tokyo, and his friend coordinated with a company in Hiroshima that made artists' brushes. The company sent Garrett brushes at a cost of 12 cents each. Sam went back to Saks and sold a whopping 36 brushes at 60 cents a piece. Saks sold them for a dollar.

Garrett's idea eventually revolutionized the cosmetic industry. He sold an order to makeup manufacturer Max Factor, and together they developed a brush for applying eye shadow, which had never been done before. He was hoping to get an order for 10,000 to 20,000 brushes. Max Factor ordered 660,000. Garrett knew that he had a winner.

"We did about 20 million a year," Garrett recalls. "I concentrated on our biggest accounts, and by the time the competition came in, I was in very solid. As time went on, the competition grew, we did not have a monopoly, but we were first."

This simple idea led to an amazing *Wow* success. It's tough to argue with those kinds of results. Garrett also believes in keeping the sales presentation simple.

"People are the same no matter where they are," he says. "Selling is simple. You don't want to talk about the product too long and lose their interest. You ask for the order. Some salespeople talk so much [that] they forget to ask for the order. It's also terribly important to have a good product. You can bluff your way once or twice, but we had a slogan: 'Never ever promise anything you can't do.'

"I treated everyone with great respect. I really didn't have to work at being their friend. I'm friendly all the time and get along with people. In fact, I'm inviting people now to my funeral even though I have a little time to go. The funeral will be at the Pebble Beach Club, and there's a new twist. We're charging a hundred dollars, and I don't want anyone there who is not sincere."

Garrett says his slogan along the way while in business was "We can sell anybody anything." We believe him, because he knows the importance of keeping it simple.

☀ HOW DO YOU GET TO CARNEGIE HALL?

Sorry, we know it's an old joke, but in the case of your elevator speech (and, for that matter, your idea itself), the punch line applies—Practice, practice, practice! Try out your idea, and your marketing pitch for it, on as many people as possible. Watch and listen for the phrases that light up their eyes (and the bulbs above their heads). Where do they make an emotional connection. When do they say, "I get it"? Use these moments as your foundation, refine your pitch, and try it on a new audience. Keep going through this process until you make it one that your audience can't resist.

When you're developing your pitch and your plan, it will be much easier—and more beneficial—to start big and narrow down than to start small. Pour out all your ideas, and then step back and begin eliminating some and subordinating others.

If your idea truly is revolutionary, it's going to be tougher to explain out loud. The listener will not have heard of such a thing before. In that case, compare it to something they do know. Out of fear of seeming less original, some naive marketers will claim, "There's never been anything like this ever." Such a claim can be more confusing than impressive. It raises more questions than it answers. Instead, compare it to something the listener does know and then explain how it takes that concept or product to a new level.

If possible, think of a story that illustrates your message. Stories are easier to remember and more engaging for the listener. Perhaps it's an anecdote about something that occurred as you developed the idea, or perhaps it's a story of how someone used what you're offering to great acclaim. The keys to a good story are that it's memorable and that it's relevant to the benefit. As people tell others the story—or see some version of it on You Tube or pass it along via e-mail—it should point them directly to what you have to sell. A story—even a funny one—that doesn't relate directly to your idea could be passed around to thousands of people, but it doesn't do you a whole lot of good unless they associate you with the story.

✳ ANTICIPATE YOUR RISKS

As you continue to work on your marketing plan, anticipate responses and objections. Why do I need this? How much will it cost in time and money? How easy is it for me to do? How is this different from what's already available?

Also anticipate what might go wrong. Of course, don't allow these possibilities to stop you from moving ahead, but do your best to foresee dangers, and be ready with solutions. In short, it pays to be paranoid. ✳

CHAPTER 7

Apply to the Present What You Learn from the Past

The best prophet of the future is the past.

—Lord Byron

It should be very clear to you by now that we believe that the secret to achieving *Wow* success is having a *Wow*. You need an idea that stands out because it is so original and because it so clearly fills a need for a specific market. Give your audience something that they've never seen before, and you'll grab their attention.

In this chapter, though, we're going to add a new layer to this advice. Even as you're developing your idea or marketing campaign that is fresh and original, be aware of what has worked—and what has failed—in the past. In other words, do you know your competition? Regardless of how successful they have been or not, they have been there and (perhaps even) done that. Think about your own career as well as about what has succeeded and failed for others.

✳ ONLY YOU

First, you. What have you done in terms of marketing in the past that has worked? It could be as simple as a well-targeted résumé to creating a multimillion-dollar ad campaign. What ingredients created that success? Did you focus your attention on networking? Did you use a unique strategy to build a buzz? Did you use an innovative technology? Did you take extra time to study your market and your competition? Did you locate a retail outlet in an ideal spot? Whatever you did, it worked. Therefore, when you launch your next idea, learn the lesson of your past success and be sure to use the strategy that worked for you in the past.

It's likely that part of the reason for the success of your strategy is that it used one of your personal strengths. If you have great communication skills and can build relationships easily, emphasizing those skills in your campaign is a good idea.

You can learn just as much—perhaps even more—from past failures. The key is a clear, honest, and in-depth assessment. This is not the time for pointing fingers, blaming others, blaming market conditions, or beating up on yourself. A sudden and untimely downturn in the marketplace can cause a lot of good ideas to fail, but step back and analyze all the contributing factors, focusing on your own contribution to the failure. Everybody who has the courage to try something difficult fails from time to time. The key is learning from your mistakes.

Just as you assessed your personal strengths and how they've led to success in the past, assess your weaknesses or the mistakes you made that led to failure. Are you a networking dynamo with no head for numbers, which led to problems in the past managing your cash flow? Did you hire people who lacked your level of passion and commitment? Did you undersell yourself in hopes of landing business and then realize you were not making the money you needed? Did you convince yourself that your idea was timely rather than taking time to analyze market trends? Whatever happened in the past, don't waste time looking for excuses. Instead, admire that you had the guts to give it a try, figure out what factors contributed to the failure, and be sure that this time you address those problems.

☀ A PANTS-SPLITTING YARN

Back in 1850, a dry-goods manufacturer named Levi Strauss headed to San Francisco to cash in on the gold rush. He brought with him a tough, durable canvas cloth and tried to sell it to make tents and wagon covers. There was no market. The gold rushers from the East had foreseen the need for tents and wagon covers and had brought what they needed. They hadn't foreseen, however, that the constant squatting next to streams while panning for the precious nuggets caused them to split their pants.

Strauss learned from his mistake and began using the durable cloth to make pants that held up a lot longer than the ones the miners had brought with them. Business boomed. He then learned from his success. He added copper rivets at the stress points in the pants, making them even harder to split. He also switched from the canvas he'd been using to a strong denim material that was more flexible and looked more stylish.

One hundred and fifty years later, we still call those jeans Levis. The lesson, of course, is to learn from both your failures and your successes. It's also important to be adaptable and to emphasize your skills. Strauss didn't throw up his hands and switch his attention to the hotel business. He knew what he knew how to do. He also knew his assets—plenty of tough canvas cloth. He assessed the needs of his market and simply found a different way to use those assets.

✳ AN IDEA TO CHEW ON

During the middle of the nineteenth century, New York inventor Thomas Adams bought a large supply of chicle from, of all people, Antonio Lopez de Santa Anna, the deposed leader of Mexico, whose name is infamous in American history books as the villain of the battle of the Alamo. He had been "exiled" to New Jersey and brought with him a huge supply of Mexican chicle, a rubbery substance extracted from sapodilla trees. Adams planned to vulcanize the chicle and sell it as a rubber substitute. He tried to use it to make toys, rain boots, tires, and a number of other products, but he failed every time. Legend has it that one day in 1869, while ruminating on his continued failures, he began chewing on a piece of chicle and was struck with the idea of using his huge supply to make a treat that would become known as *chewing gum*. This is a wonderfully dramatic story, but it's more likely that he knew that the practice of chewing chicle wasn't uncommon in certain areas of Mexico and among Native Americas.

Nevertheless, he took the idea a step further. He boiled some of his supply and began offering it to stores in his neighborhood. Soon he added flavor to the chicle, and within a year, he invented a machine that would produce his treat in large quantities. In early 1871, his factory began producing Adams New York Gum. From there, Adams built what would become a chewing-gum empire, boasting such brands as Black Jack, Clove, and Beeman's that remained popular for a hundred years.

We're not saying that the next time you're stuck on where to go with an idea, you might want to stick it in your mouth, but the Adams story is a classic tale of ingenuity—of seeing failures as stepping stones to success.

✳ THE WHEEL HAS BEEN INVENTED

Yes, your idea must be original, but very often the best ideas give a new spin to something that already exists. The things we buy and use today evolved from things our parents used, which evolved from . . . well, you get the idea. The personal computers in most homes today evolved from the technology of big mainframe computers that 50 years ago were found at major corporations and government agencies.

Brian Kurtz is the executive vice president of Boardroom, Inc., a newsletter and book publisher with millions of subscribers and book buyers. Boardroom's *Bottom Line/Personal* newsletter is one of America's most popular general consumer newsletters. While traditional publishers hope to sell 50,000 copies of a book, Boardroom sells hundreds of thousands of copies through direct marketing. The company has become famous for its innovative marketing campaigns.

Kurtz is a firm believer in learning from the past. "You have to realize that it has all been invented before, even when you're being the inventor," he says.

"I'm not a genius, and I'm not thinking of breakthrough ideas every minute. It's like the old joke: What do you call the person who finished last in his class at Harvard Medical School?"

The punchline: "Doctor."

The secret to success, Kurtz says, is to look for successful models and adapt them to your own needs. "It's not about reinventing the wheel. Innovation is a matter of building on a variety of things. Not every idea has to be a breakthrough."

Too often we strive to be so creative that we lose sight of what has worked before and how a new approach can turn something familiar into something original. We're not talking about a "me too" approach here. We're saying that you often can find your *Wow* by examining what has worked in the past and adding a new element. Or you can examine what failed in the past and figure out if adding a new element will turn that failure into *Wow* success.

"*Wows* don't all have to be homeruns," Kurtz says. "A lot of businesses are built on singles and doubles. When you start building on them, they can end up a homerun." Kurtz feels that the dot-com craze fed a "homerun mentality" that with the dot-com bust has been tempered in business today.

We've all seen what can happen when the quest for the next new thing is not accompanied by a real need in the marketplace. At the beginning of the dot-com craze, companies were terrified of losing market share and being left behind in the frenzy to stick one's flag into the new land of the Internet. Companies grasped in all directions and grabbed what seemed new while forgetting about their core business and what had worked for them in the past.

The collapse of the dot-com bubble taught us all a lesson, and if we're smart, we'll remember that lesson. When we learn from failures as well as from the successes of others, we can gain wisdom while avoiding the hardships.

"I think every company will go through that homerun mentality at some point," Kurtz says. "Or the opposite—you think it's a homerun when it really isn't. You'll be more successful not trying to do everything at once. Build it slowly. I'm a big believer in serendipity, in putting out positive energy in a lot of directions. When you do that, good things are going to happen."

☀ CHEESEHEAD WISDOM

Examine the success of players in other industries. In an article in *Dairy Business*, Jerry Dryer, president of J/D/G Consulting, a dairy marketing, communications, and forecasting company, exhorts milk producers to learn a lesson from the success of fellow dairy dynamos selling cheese.

"Per-capita sales have about tripled," he writes. "And many of the reasons for cheese's remarkable sales pace are lessons milk marketers need to learn. Unlike their buddies in the milk business with few product varieties and fewer package choices, cheeseheads have capitalized on hundreds of cheese varieties and put them into dozens of package sizes, shapes, and colors with lots of configurations (e.g., chunks, shreds, slices, cubes, and spreads)."

Whether you're a small-business owner, a one-person operation, or a manager in a large company, think about what successful elements—whether it's packaging or design or whatever—you can adapt to your own idea to give it an extra *Wow*? Look around you. What's working in the world of business today? How can you use a similar approach in your own market?

☀ A SPACE OF ONE'S OWN

In 2003, a social networking Web site called MySpace was launched and quickly drew hundreds of thousands of users, especially teenagers. Now a well-known part of the teen scene, it gave them a space through which they could contact friends and meet new ones. They could design their space to make a personal statement—sort of a virtual room. By 2006, it boasted a hundred million users.

It was most popular among high school students and is now almost synonymous with them. In 2004, Mark Zuckerburg, a student at Harvard, decided that his college pals needed a social networking platform of their own. The network quickly expanded to the entire campus, then to nearby universities, and then throughout the Ivy League. The idea was similar to MySpace, but it appealed to an older audience, initially college students eager to shrug off anything that smacked of high school.

Today, Facebook is has the largest number of registered users among college-focused sites with over 34 million active members worldwide. It is the sixth most visited Web site on the Internet, and experts are calling it the catalyst for a whole new way of using Internet communications. Zuckerburg and college buddies didn't create the idea out of thin air. They found a new market for a model that was already popular.

☀ ON-AIR BUD

A recent innovative marketing campaign that's been far less successful can be found on Bud TV. Actually, it *is* Bud TV. Launched a couple of years ago for a reported $35 million, the online network hoped to cash in on the success of new technologies and the movement to mix marketing messages with creative content. After a splashy debut and lots of media buzz, however, viewer interest faded. Some of the commercials made the rounds on You Tube, particularly one for Bud Light that told the story of office workers who created a "curse jar," each worker paying a fine to the jar every time they cursed. When they decide to use the money to buy Bud Light for an office party, the curse words fly. They're "beeped out," of course, but the results are hilarious. The commercial seemed to be passed around electronically to every office in the country.

Unfortunately, Bud TV turned out to miss its mark. It offered a number of original shows, including one featuring sports announcer Jack Buck doing interviews in a New York cab, but audiences assumed that the content mostly involved beer. The marketing message wasn't clear, and it wasn't spread widely enough to generate interest itself. The interest remained largely in the innovative platform. Also, in a number of states, attorneys general insisted on strict registration controls so that the online station didn't promote underage drinking. The registration process ended up being so cumbersome and annoying that fewer and fewer viewers signed up.

A costly mistake? Maybe. It's too soon to know. To the company's credit, Anheuser Busch looked around and saw what had succeeded in the marketplace and hoped to create its own viral-marketing campaign. The company had seen the growth of You Tube and Facebook and other sites that were attracting the attention of millions of people. Its marketing effort was gutsy and innovative.

The lesson is in making sure that all the layers are working together. An innovative idea without a clear and simple message may fail to spark interest. A large market isn't much good to you if you don't know how to reach it.

You can learn from this example, continuing to refine your own plan and taking the time to examine each layer, ensuring that they complement each other. When they do, you're on your way to *Wow* success. ✳

CHAPTER 8

Create Alliances

I have found no greater satisfaction than achieving success through honest dealing and strict adherence to the view that, for you to gain, those you deal with should gain as well.

—Alan Greenspan

Songwriter Paul Simon sang about being a "rock" and an "island"– a sentiment suited perfectly to teen angst but not one to use on your way to *Wow* success. You need all the help you can get. Our advice: seek it. As we discuss in Chapter 13, tell everyone you know about what you're doing. You never know how someone might know someone who knows someone who knows someone who can offer you a big boost. Don't discount any opportunity. We've found in our experience that sometimes the most likely sources fail to deliver, whereas unexpected sources appear out of the blue.

More to the point for this chapter–begin actively creating alliances with others who have goals of their own, people who can help you reach your goals while you help them reach theirs. Create synergies that are mutually beneficial, and you'll find that the road to *Wow* success is a whole lot easier.

Recall Jack Canfield's story in Chapter 1 about the woman from the bookstore chain who helped him to sell 1 million books in a single day. Reaching that goal helped both of them, and neither could have done it without the other. Take every opportunity to find people with whom you can create an alliance.

✳ FUSING, TYING, COLLABORATING

"One of the most rewarding, inexpensive, underused, and effective methods of marketing is to tie in your marketing efforts with the efforts of others," writes Jay Conrad Levinson on his Web site gmarketing.com. The author of many books on guerilla marketing, Levinson believes in the power of a mutual hitching of wagons to reach for the stars. We agree. Obviously! This book is a case in point. We've written a number of books together and know first hand the benefits of creating an alliance.

A common term for this approach is *fusion marketing*, and the strategy is used by corporations big and small as well as by savvy entrepreneurs who want to expand the reach of their resources and share contacts. Think about who you know or might meet who could help you and who you could help at the same time. Never miss a chance to be with smart, creative people connected to the world you want to reach. In turn, be generous with your time and resources to help them.

✳ TEAMWORK TO MAKE THE DREAM WORK

Sandra Yancey is the CEO and founder of the eWomenNetwork, a highly impressive gathering of women on the Internet and one of the fastest-growing membership-based professional women's networking organizations in North America. It's a leading resource for connecting and promoting women and their businesses worldwide. Along with her husband, Kym, she also created the eWomenNetwork Foundation, a nonprofit arm of the network designed to help support the financial and emotional health of women and children in need. Yancey attributes her success to her belief that we must "give first, share always," and through that belief she has formed many relationships that have helped her to achieve her goals.

"Connecting with success is all about the people you have in your life that you value, care for, and enrich," she says. "However, the flip side of the coin is all the phenomenal people you have yet to meet and the people you don't even know yet. Ultimately, knowing the right people can help solve the majority of our problems. Perhaps you need more cash flow, you need good financial people, or you need a good banker. It's all about knowing people and creating relationships. Life is about relationships. Alliances have helped me be successful because they've given me access to needed resources when I've benefited to grow professionally and personally. They've been there to support me in times of great joy as well as overcoming hurdles. I think we have an obligation in life that 'you cannot expect others to do for you what you are not first willing to do for other people.' In other words, how can I have hoped to create a relationship for me if I don't help you?"

Since its inception, the eWomenNetwork, with the help of members and other strategic alliances, has awarded hundreds of thousands of dollars in cash grants, in-kind donations, and support to women's nonprofit organizations and emerging female leaders of tomorrow. Yancey was featured on CNN's *Anderson Cooper 360* as an American hero for her role in mobilizing much-needed resources for the girl's high school basketball team of Pass Christian, Mississippi, in the wake of the Hurricane Katrina devastation. Alliances helped to make it happen and continue to be critical to Yancey's company and foundation.

"Our networking organization is first and foremost a loyal, dedicated community of women-owned businesses, corporate professionals, and entrepreneurs who want to support and network with other dynamic women. When we created our company, we designed an exclusive trademarked brand of Accelerated Networking events occurring in cities all across the United States and Canada. We have pioneered a whole new way for women to build relationships and transact business. The eWomenNetwork offers a safe and secure Internet environment that allows women to connect and network with each other across cyberspace and represents a whole new approach which honors how women connect, collaborate, and create with each other.

"Women experience real relationship building focusing on what you are giving versus receiving. However, once you give freely and unconditionally, you end up on the receiving side. Immediate results emerge while our members participate in fast-tracked networking dinners. Each member addresses what she is selling as well as purchasing in the next 30 days. Alliances are formed instantly, and an exchange of business cards happens in lightning-strike speed."

Sandra's motto is "It's not about *me*; it's about *we*. It takes teamwork to make the dream work."

✳ ROBYN CREATES ALLIANCES

After reading *Life's Little Instruction Book*, I was so moved by H. Jackson Brown's compilation of observations written for his son Adam, who was heading off to college, that I recommended it to everyone. Brown's instructions for a rewarding life touched me in such a profound manner that I wanted to talk to this author. I was so impressed with his "kitchen table philosopher" approach, as he referred to himself, that I called him and introduced myself. Then I began calling him from the carpool line while I waited for my kids to get out of school. In fact, I called him weekly to say hello for months. Fortunately, I was not perceived as a stalker, and he welcomed my calls and took a sincere and generous interest in the books I was writing.

After weeks of getting up the courage to dial his number, I asked if he'd ever consider writing a book with me. He replied, "Tell me a book I might like, and I'll consider it." Looking back, I have to say it was quite a gutsy thing for me to do at the time. Who did I think I was to invite a *New York Times* best-selling author to coauthor a book with someone who he hardly knew? As the weeks passed and Jack listened to my ideas, one remarkable day he said, "Robyn, I think you might have something."

We ultimately wrote two books together—*Life's Little Instruction Book for Incurable Romantics* and *A Hero in Every Heart*. Working with H. Jackson Brown,

Jr., was my good fortune, and we formed a wonderful partnership on those projects. In addition, my husband and I formed a friendship with Jack and his wonderful wife, Rosemary, that we treasure. Without my extreme persistence and being prepared to overdeliver, it would have never happened. However, the value of working with Jack Brown soared far past the actual books because working with someone of his extreme talent, focus, and amazing insight into what matters in life was a gift I'll forever value. He also taught me by example how to become a smarter author and a smart business woman. Hitting the ball out of the ballpark was his view of a home run! Jack continues to be my literary hero and a generous supporter of my work. Whoever says the carpool line is a waste of time is missing the minivan!

Throughout my career, I've spotted many individuals doing something really amazing that wowed me. For example, I was very impressed with Dr. Stephen Garber, a behavioral psychologist, and his wife, Dr. Marianne Garber, an educational consultant. The Garbers were helping a friend's child who had some learning problems, and I was very impressed with the work they were doing. As a new mom with a rambunctious two-year-old at home, I knew that I needed, like all parents, the best information and advice I could find. When I couldn't find an updated book at the bookstore, I approached the Garbers to help me write a book on childhood behavior entitled, *Good Behavior*, that ultimately became my first of many hardcover books.

The book sparked a national tour, endless interviews, and outstanding reviews, and it became the cornerstone of my book-writing career. Over 25 years later, the book is still in print. However, to make that book a *Wow*, we brainstormed with the parents of young children—developing a list of hundreds of behaviors their children were doing, including hitting, spitting, biting, fighting, won't take no for an answer, won't go to bed at night, and many other concerns. When we finished the proposal, we had a list that required a monumental effort.

The Garbers proved my initial impressions to be correct, and we worked together for three years on the book. It was a true collaborative effort in which our writing styles and ideas merged into a united effort to help parents solve the common and not so common problems associated with raising a family. The *Wow* about our relationship was that working together we wowed each other with the ideas, knowledge, and writing skills we all brought to the table. Twenty-five years later, our book still continues to help families.

When we finished it, we had the amazing pleasure of being in a bidding war with three offers from the top publishers in the country. We set out to write the definitive book on childhood behavior and made it happen with the help of our literary agent Meredith Bernstein. While I didn't have a Ph.D., I was a creative idea person and a mom in the trenches, and I had a valuable perspective.

The Garbers and I wrote many books together over the years, from *Good Behavior* to *Monsters Under the Bed* (on childhood fears) to *Beyond Ritalin* (on attention-deficit disorder), and the books have helped parents around the world. Our work was nominated for a better life award and was recommended by *USA Today* as one of the top parenting books every parent needs.

Another story illustrates this law well. When I was invited to attend—as an author and media personality to sign 200 books that I had written—a new career fair called Women For Hire that was happening in Atlanta at a large convention center, I certainly was motivated and inclined to go. Here was someone purchasing and giving away 200 of my books for free, and it was just an hour of my time.

However, when I arrived, I saw lines wrapped around the building. Thousands of women had come to network for a job. It deeply struck a chord with me because I felt such compassion for these deserving women. As I signed the books, I noticed that many of these talented women were fumbling with résumés, some were not dressed appropriately, and others needed help presenting themselves. The career fair, however—conceived, owned, and operated by Tory Johnson—was outstanding. It was inspiring to see someone helping such capable, smart, deserving women get jobs, grow professionally, and connect with leading corporations. I knew right then and there that I wanted to meet and thank Johnson. After signing the books, I went up to Johnson, introduced myself, raved about her event, and without any hesitation asked her if she wanted to write a book with me on helping women get jobs. Tory enthusiastically said yes, and to date, we have written three books, including *Take This Book to Work*, that help women to get ahead in the workplace by asking smart questions.

When you have passion, drive, and ability, and if you know what you are good at or simply what you enjoy doing most, put those talents to work by finding people to work with who share your goal. Whether it's working from home, starting a business, finding meaningful employment, or putting your company on the map in a huge way, surround yourself with people who bring to the table something extraordinary.

☀ IT'S YOUR BUSINESS

While we're talking about Tory Johnson, we should point out that she's made many strong and highly impressive alliances of her own. After being fired from her publicity job at NBC News, where she worked for superstars including Jane Pauley, Maria Shriver, and Tim Russert, and being told by the news division president that "it's a big world out there—go explore it," Johnson picked herself up after a self-described week-long pity party and did just that. She came up with an idea that eventually became her passion in life, one that illustrates how powerful and freeing the idea of owning your own business can be—especially if you're willing to take a chance, trust your instincts, and work like crazy.

Johnson's idea was to start a company that produced career fairs for women. Even though career fairs were a dime a dozen, nothing existed specifically for women. And seeing that diversity in the corporate world is a growing priority—and because women face special challenges in launching and advancing their careers—Johnson thought that if she could connect women with good employers, she would have a win-win-win situation.

Today, after founding Women For Hire in 1999 in a bedroom of her Manhattan apartment, with dozens of career fairs behind her and many more to come, having connected thousands of women with hundreds of top employers, Johnson and her company, Women For Hire, are definite winners.

Why? Because empowering women is the most rewarding professional goal Johnson could ever dream of. To get the word out about her company and its mission, Johnson did everything from cold calling executives to convince them to support her career expos to giving speeches and pitching herself to local television, radio, and print outlets. As she expanded Women For Hire from one city, New York, to 10 other major cities, she encouraged women to attend her free career expos, and she educated them on how to maximize their potential for success. The media took note, as did more than 1,500 top employers ranging from IBM to the FBI, and her events continue to soar.

"If you really want to be successful and break through the noise—whether in the corporate world or as an entrepreneur, don't expect anyone else to pump up your passion—you've got to have it in your heart and in your head on your own," Johnson says.

She adds that it's essential to align yourself with people who lift you up. "Think of those who are smarter than you, wiser, kinder, and funnier. Go to them for advice, seek their counsel, listen to their inspiration and encouragement." But, she warns, "Never, ever ignore your gut. After all, it's your business."

When Johnson's kids, Jake and Emma, began preschool, one of their classmates was Michael, a cute kid whose mom happens to be Kelly Ripa. The kids got friendly, and so did the moms, and Ripa took an interest in Johnson's work. The result: three fabulous launch parties hosted by Ripa to support Johnson's career books that were cowritten with Robyn, tons of on-air plugs about Women For Hire, and a solid friendship among the working moms. Tory's not bragging. Rather, she says, "Networking—reaching out to family and friends who can help you, and building and nurturing those relationships wherever and however they originate—is nothing to be ashamed of."

Today, Johnson appears regularly on ABC's *Good Morning America* as the workplace contributor, reaching millions of morning show viewers. When it's working with a mom looking to make a career comeback after time off or a seasoned professional eyeing her next corporate move, Johnson remains passionate about spreading her mission of empowering women all over the country to achieve their personal and professional best.

✳ ROBYN'S SON'S ALLIANCE

When my son Justin, who is now an attorney, attended law school, he wished he had been able to find a book that informed him about what insiders who have been there knew about surviving law school. And so, after he graduated, he decided to write a book to help other first-year law students learn from the mistakes and experiences of others. He wrote *The Insider's Guide to Your First Year of Law School: A Student-to-Student Handbook from a Law School Survivor* (Adams Media, 2007). When he finished the book, he decided to pursue George H. Ross, executive vice president and senior counsel of the Trump Organization, inviting George Ross to write his Foreword. He wanted to align with someone other students admired.

Asking for a cover blurb would have been gutsy for this law school student. However, Justin thought a foreword would be most meaningful from George Ross, who not only costarred in *The Apprentice* but also was an NYU professor teaching the art of negotiation, as well as with having authored two best-sellers, including *Trump Style Negotiation* and *Trump Strategies for Real Estate*. He also practiced law for more than 50 years, closing multimillion-dollar deals for Donald Trump, and served as business adviser, legal counsel, and negotiator for the leading real estate owners and developers in New York City.

Since Ross's success started in a crowded classroom at Brooklyn Law School, he knew what it was like to be in a beginning law student's shoes. In his Foreword, which he graciously agreed to do, he wrote, "Justin Spizman's book is a great resource for incoming law students. If I'd had a book like this when I started my first year, I would have avoided plenty of needless headaches and aggravation." Not only did Justin score a foreword, but he had the generous support of a brilliant, experienced lawyer who clearly could trump anyone in business. Not bad for a brand-new attorney and first-time author.

✳ THE POWER OF ALLIANCE

Look at any issue of a national business magazine or Web site and you'll find out about the latest alliance between big corporations. Whether it's a one-time cross-promotion or a joint venture slated to continue indefinitely, executives know the value of sharing resources to reach a particular market. The risk, of course, is that the partnership will sour, that one or both parties will feel they're getting the short end of the marketing stick. The power of the alliance, however, is generated by uniting the equity both brands or both parties bring to the partnership. The key, of course, is that both sides benefit from the synergy. Another important element to consider is the fit—how well the skills, reputation, and resources of each party work together.

Back in the early 2000s, for example, Wrigley's launched its Orbit gum brand by forming an alliance with Crest toothpaste, owned by Proctor & Gamble (P&G). While a partnership between chewing gum and toothpaste sounds like a dentist's worst nightmare, things have worked out well. A new product was created, Orbit Whitening Gum "powered by Crest." In an article for Interbrand's Brand Channel Web site, Bryan McCleary, P&G's global brand manager of external relations for P&G's oral-care brands, says, "We could have worked on—and actually did work on—bringing our own gum to market with Crest branding. But we came to the realization that that wasn't our core area of expertise and that if we really wanted to create a great product, we needed someone who had great experience within the product category, with gums and flavors and taste and production—and also had great distribution networks for gum. We didn't have those things, but we did have great knowledge of the oral-care business."

The result? Orbit is now one of the top five chewing gums in the country and is, according to *Chicago* magazine, "an industry-shattering success."

So find an ally that fits, marshall your collective assets and resources, and reach for the *Wow*. ✳

CHAPTER 9

Hire People Smarter than You

First-rate people hire first-rate people; second-rate people
hire third-rate people.

—Leo Rosten

Y ou really know you're in business when the time comes to hire
someone to help you with it. Congratulations. That's a key milestone
on your way to *Wow* success. Most of the largest, successful businesses on
earth have been started by one person who hired another person. Who will
you hire? Our advice: hire people who are smarter than you. By this we mean
hire people whose skills set is different from yours, who enlarge and expand
your efforts to achieve success. Are you a creative thinker but poorly organ-
ized? You need someone who thinks in a linear way and can keep the operation running smoothly. Are you an introverted inventor? You need someone
who is outgoing and can sell what you make. Low tech? Get someone who
isn't. As billionaire Donald Trump observed, "You can't know it all. No matter
how smart you are, no matter how comprehensive your education, no matter
how wide ranging your experience, there is simply no way to acquire all the
wisdom you need to make your business thrive."

Too often we see companies crippled by not giving enough time and
attention to this crucial law of marketing. The best companies hire smart, passionate, motivated people who take a sense of ownership in the mission.

There's an old saying, attributed to at least a half dozen corporate gurus,
that goes something like this: "Hire great people, and then get out of the way."
It's an old saying because it's true. (Sayings not based in truth tend to fade
away while they're still young.) Great people still need guidance, but don't be

afraid to create for them a creative, dynamic environment in which they can flourish. Those who are afraid to hire people who know things they don't and who can do things they can't might as well do everything themselves.

As motivational speaker and former college head coach Lou Holtz once said, "It's not my job to motivate players. They bring extraordinary motivation to our program. It's my job not to demotivate them." If you have to spend a lot of time motivating someone, you've chosen the wrong person. If the person came to you motivated and has lost his or her edge, that person has chosen the wrong boss.

✳ THE RIGHT PEOPLE

Michael Hutchinson has spent many years hiring people, recruiting them, and matching them to the right jobs. A successful author, speaker, and CEO of Make Results Happen, he knows how to put people in positions where they can succeed.

In 1986, Hutchinson began to work with motivational speaker Anthony Robbins and helped to build the enormously successful business now known throughout the world. Hutchinson helped to design seminars and brought in big-name speakers to address specific topics. He also hired promoters and sales reps to increase awareness and to sell the program.

"It's all about being around the right people," he says. "It's about getting the right people on the team, making the right decisions. My success has been putting my focus on my customer, my recruit, or whatever. If I felt in my gut that what I have is right for them, I'm a bulldog in seeing them get what they want." With Hutchinson's able assistance, the name Tony Robbins grew as big as Robbins himself. Hutchinson says simply, "I provided the direction, and Tony was the torrent, the mighty river."

Determining which people are the right ones is not an exact science, and even for a seasoned professional, it can be difficult to explain.

"You ask yourself: Can they do the job? Do they want to do the job? Does it fit with their personal goals?" Hutchinson says. "The rest is just an intuition, a gut feeling. I've made poor decisions in my life. There are so many lessons, and I've made so many mistakes. It's like the old saying about good judgment being the result of bad mistakes. The more you learn, the more you take advantage of training and personal development, the more you grow, the more valuable you become to somebody else. Always be growing, working harder on yourself. If you're not growing, you're dying. I see that in the business world as well as in personal life."

✳ PEOPLE WITH PASSION

Edie Fraser is managing partner and diversity chair of the largest woman-owned executive search firm, Diversified Search Ray & Berndtson. She has hired many people during her career, and she believes that passion in life is everything. She is an internationally acclaimed corporate executive, champion and advocate for diversity and women, and an advocate for the advancement of minorities and women.

"Start with the *P*s for success," she says, "and see if you agree on what you need to achieve it all: passion, performance, positive style, persuasion, partnering, persistence, and a people orientation. Passion—either you have it or you don't succeed. It is a necessity, and you need positive people around you. Stay positive as negativity only makes it worse. Surround yourself with those that are positive sources. Stay away from negativity or, as Maya Angelou says, 'Get rid of those who are whiners.' When you visualize success, success happens. Of course, it doesn't happen overnight, but a positive mental attitude is the elixir of a meaningful life. And life is about giving. Gratitude is an attitude. Give thanks several times a day."

Some of her strong beliefs in addition to passion are to use the power of persuasion. "Believe what you say, and you will persuade with a natural ease because you believe," she advises. "There are risks and rewards, and both are worth the opportunity to win and apply to advancement. Partner. Build relationships and partnerships internally and externally. We can't do it alone. Mentor and give freely in this regard. Persistence. Be persistent as there is no alternative to success. Add a shake of perseverance. Don't be afraid to fail as we all do. Build with positive people internally and externally. People make it happen."

✳ RICK'S RULES

If I've hired 500 people in my life, I've screwed up on five. I've been very blessed, but there are a couple of rules I follow to help bring on the right people for the job. Most important, I want them to be passionate and energetic, and they have to be positive people. This is more important than just having experience in a certain area. I once hired a young woman whose previous job was selling pretzels. What interested me was where she sold them—at the bottom of the Tower of Terror at Disneyworld. The Disney people are amazing. So anyone who has worked there successfully has a wonderful attitude. She became one of my best publicists. It's like the old Vince Lombardi line, "If you're not fired with enthusiasm, you will be fired with enthusiasm."

If you have a negative person in your company, that person becomes a cancer. You must get that person out of your company immediately. Negativity spreads like wildfire. I've hired people who had a lot to learn, but they brought a lot of positive energy to the job. They were team players. I've had a few who just didn't work well with other people. One woman liked to use words that nobody ever knew just to show that she was smart or well educated. It didn't work out. Even though she was smart, she wasn't a team player. It's sandbox mentality. If you can't play well, I don't care how smart you are.

I always had the philosophy that Rick's way isn't the best way. If your idea is better, let's do it that way. I truly believe that my hires are smarter than I am in the things I hired them to do, and I listen to them. They have different areas of expertise, and I respect that fact. That's why I hired them. If we're partners and do the same thing, one of us isn't needed.

One way I test the passion and interest of my hires in the position is to find out how much research they've done before the job interview. Have they been on the Web site? Have they read some of the things I've written? Have they taken time to find out what we do and how we do it? If they don't know that I have a cockapoo named Rusty, the chances are they're not going to get hired. I mention Rusty at the end of all the pieces on the site.

If you're smart enough and passionate enough about the job to have done your homework, you'll know that. It has served me pretty well. ✳

CHAPTER 10

Customize Customer Service

A lot of people think that the new economy is all about the
Internet. I think that it's being fueled by the Internet . . .
but that it's really about customers.

—Patricia Seybold

A ri Weinzweig, cofounder and co-owner of Zingerman's Deli in Ann
Arbor, Michigan, recalls one of his managers waiting at the front
door for customers to arrive on a rainy night. At Zingerman's Roadhouse
sit-down restaurant location, umbrellas are kept at the service stand so that
servers can walk customers to their cars in the rain after their meal. But
Joanie, one of the managers, took that commitment to service one step further
by standing at the front door waiting for cars pulling into the parking lot. She
ran out to the cars with an umbrella to walk the customers into the restaurant.
Now that's customer service! You've made friends even before your diners step
foot in the place.

Amazing. But at Zingerman's—all in a day's work. This is the approach
taken by everyone who works there. In fact, Zingerman's is so well known for
customer service that Weinzweig published a book about it: *Zingerman's Guide
to Giving Great Service—Treating Your Customers Like Royalty.* Weinzweig
opened the deli in 1982 with business partner Paul Saginaw. Since then, they've
become famous for a lot more than their corned beef and pastrami sandwiches
(which are to die for, by the way). They're known for the way they treat their
customers. And because of the way they treat their customers, they've got a
lot of them. Those customers are loyal to the place, coming back time and

again for the wonderful food and service. In the Ann Arbor area, any visit by an out-of-towner wouldn't be complete without a stop at Zingerman's.

✳ CUSTOMIZE YOUR SERVICE

Customers today have high expectations. They enjoy such a multitude of purchase options that they expect customized, personal service. They want to feel special and unique because, frankly, too often businesses fail to make them feel that way. Think of your own consumer experiences. When you call about a product or service, are you greeted by a recording offering you a menu of numbers to press, which only leads you to a new menu with more numbers to press? How loyal do you feel to that company? How important do you feel?

Customers, as we've said, want to know what's in it for them, and to create loyal customers, you have to give them more than just a bang for their buck. You have to give them a *big bang*. The good news is that so many companies fail to deliver, so when you *do* deliver, customers notice.

Go beyond courtesy. Customize your customer service, listening to and even intuiting each customer's needs. To reach *Wow* success, you need to target your customers' needs even before they've been expressed. To be distinctive, be instinctive.

"Every customer is different, and you need to reengage each customer," Weinzweig says. "Our philosophy of customer service is of value to anyone in the service industry of any sort large or small. We define great service with three steps: First, figure out what the customer would like; second, get it for them; and third, go the extra mile. If you use these three steps, they work. These customer service steps have been used in many organizations including everything from health care to libraries to legal firms, universities, nonprofits, for-profits, [and] by booksellers and large corporations."

This is a simple plan, sure, but it is one that very few businesses seem able to execute consistently. If they did, Zingerman's would not be seen as quite so special. Zingerman's goes the extra mile on a daily basis, and as we all know, that's not easy. Every business can go beyond expectations once in a while, but dedicating yourself to doing it every day and with every customer is what's necessary to set yourself apart.

"Each customer wants and deserves a great experience," Weinzweig says. "They don't care about how great service was the other 99 times; the service has to be great today. When we do this work well, we deliver better experiences to everybody, and the quality of the workplace is better, and the customer's experience is better, and the world is slightly better for all of us as well."

The key is in the approach employees at Zingerman's have been trained to take every time they take an order or greet a customer. Again—easier said than done.

"At Zingermans, we want to engage them and spend enough time with the customers, not as little as possible," says Weinzweig. "More time talking, not less. Then we can meet their needs. You have to really listen. Each customer interaction is a unique experience. And then if they want something, we get it for them. We do so with accuracy, politeness, and enthusiasm. We define that as doing something for the guests that they didn't ask us to do and in essence it leads to the *Wow*!

"Everyone in our organization is authorized to make things right for a customer and do whatever they need to do. You make a customer for life out of little things with a big impact. If our food or service wasn't good, we wouldn't make the customer for life, so those have to be good, too, but in my 30 years of business, I've seen that the concept of customer service is that you build one customer at a time, and we need to do a great job with our recipe for success."

✳ CUPPA COMFORT

Starbucks, without a doubt, serves a good cup of coffee. But it's the way the company serves it that has taken the company from a single location in

Seattle to a multimillion-dollar business and one of the most recognized brands in the country. To create that kind of growth, you need to offer a whole lot more than a good cup of coffee.

Starbucks developed a system that made every employee feel connected to the business. With this mind-set, every employee works to make every customer feel part of Starbuck's too. And like the folks at Zingerman's, Starbucks' "partners" (the word used within the company for all employees to emphasize the shared connection to the company's success) go the extra mile.

In his best-selling book, *The Starbucks Experience: 5 Principles for Turning Ordinary into Extraordinary*, author Joseph A. Michelli details the company's emphasis on customer service—going the extra mile to make every person who walks into a Starbucks location feel special. One way the company goes the extra mile is by continuing to surprise customers with service far beyond what's expected. Michelli writes about an unadvertised promotion in which employees gave away 1 million free cups of ice cream to celebrate National Ice Cream Month. Starbucks sells ice cream, but only in supermarkets, not at its own locations. The giveaway simply provided a means to surprise customers with an unexpected treat.

"Starbucks is not in the coffee business serving people, they're in the people business serving coffee," Michelli says. "It's a complete shift. What they've created is a place, an environment, where people want to go."

Michelli also has written about customer service in *When Fish Fly: Lessons for Creating a Vital and Energized Workplace*, which he coauthored with the Pike Place Fish Market in Seattle, and in an upcoming book with the Ritz-Carlton Company. He sees similarities in all these businesses in terms of customer service.

☀ DING!

How does a low-fare, no-frills regional airline grow into the largest in the country? Southwest Airlines carries more domestic passengers per year than any other airline, and it ranks sixth in total revenue. For 35 years in a row, Southwest has made a profit, a huge accomplishment in an industry where bankruptcy is far more common than bank deposits.

Southwest's success has been based largely on innovative business strategies and truly exceptional customer service. In 1973, Southwest instituted the first profit-sharing plan in U.S. airline history, and employees now own approximately 10 percent of the company. With that sense of ownership, employees approach their jobs—and their customers—with energy and interest. They give everything they do a personal touch, and they add a touch of humor too.

Flying in the post-9/11 world is a less pleasant experience than ever. But rather than add to the misery—or just ignore it—Southwest strives to make the trip as pleasant as possible, and the results show in customer loyalty and the bottom line. The company's TV commercials are cued to the recognizable "ding" of an airplane intercom. Of course, all marketers would love to spark some type of Pavlovian response from customers with such a sound. Southwest hasn't quite managed to make the response automatic, but it helps to reinforce the playful, positive brand identity that the company has developed by customizing its customer service.

"Great customer service is memorable, unique, and transformational," Michelli says. "By 'transformational,' I mean that by the time you leave, something has shifted in you as a result of the experience. You don't leave the same way you came in. You're feeling better. If it's the Pike Place Fish Market, you take a dead, cold, slimy fish and turn it into a playful experience. If it's Starbucks, you have an ordinary, even dull product, a cup of coffee, and you create an exceptional experience. If it's the Ritz-Carlton, it's all staged around the memorable experience.

Adequate customer service is not enough if you want to create customer loyalty and stand out in the marketplace. "Doing what's expected is only the ticket to the dance," Michelli says. "Doing what's expected gets you customers who are just a coupon away from going somewhere else. Serving a quality hamburger in itself isn't enough. You have to create that memorable experience to differentiate yourself. Basic service, doing what's expected, is a commodity."

✳ SERVICE WITH HEART

A crucial part of customer service is sincerity. Even when you're tired and trying to do three things at once, respond to each customer or each person in your marketing campaign with gratitude. That person could just as easily be a loyal customer of your competition. Instead, the person has chosen you. He or she has a need for your product or service and has asked if you can fill that need, if you can provide a solution. If you're truly passionate about what you have to offer, then you should be passionate about offering it. Offer it with passion, with sincerity, with a genuine desire to help, and you will create more than a happy customer. And you'll feel pretty darn good yourself.

"Whatever you do, do with all your heart," says Mark Sanborn, author of the international beloved best-seller, *The Fred Factor*. "It's not the job but the person doing the job that makes it extraordinary. Start where you are at."

In *The Fred Factor*, Sanborn tells the delightful and moving real-life story of a mail carrier who truly loves his job and cares about the people on his delivery route. He watches the houses and knows when people are away on trips. He finds no end of ways to deliver a lot more than the mail. He delivers kindness and attention to detail. Rather than viewing his job as dull or inconsequential, he takes pride in it and continually goes the extra mile.

As an example, he mentions Martha Stewart. "She proved that someone who decorated for the holidays, cooked for her family, and loved entertaining and doing crafts was important. Someone else might be complaining of those daily routines. She put what she was good at right at the height of her consciousness." Bob Danzig, who is now the CEO of Hurst Corporation, started his career in the mailroom. He's now retired and gives the proceeds from his speeches to charity. Bob was an orphan and has a great love for orphans, but while in the mailroom, he could have just said, "I'm just pushing mail around." Bob didn't know Sanborn's Fred the mail carrier, but the principle is the same and timeless. Go beyond what's expected. Do it every day. And do it because it makes you feel good.

"Good things come into your life when you do good things," says Sanborn. "You attract good things by doing good things. The only way to short circuit doing good is to have an ulterior motive. All I know is that the people who introduce us with an incentive end up just doing business. In life, you can be transactional or focused on the relationship. When people build a relationship, it's not like an ATM, where you stick a card in and money pops up. If you do it expecting something, you are working with the inferior motivation. Fred is still delivering the mail. That's what he wants to do, and he does it with all his heart."

✳ IT'S ALL ABOUT THE LAYERS

As should be growing clearer, the laws of *Wow* success work in harmony. The layers you put in place mingle with and augment each other in a synergy that makes each one stronger. Customer service, for example, is crucial, as we've discussed in this chapter. To supply that service, you have to know your customers and think benefit. To ensure that you're supplying a high level of customer service, you need to hire the right people—those who share your passion and your drive for the goal. ✳

PART  3

Wire Yourself
for Success

CHAPTER 11

Build One Layer at a Time

You will either step forward into growth or you will step back into safety.

—Abraham Maslow

In the Introduction, we mentioned making a lasagna, which was a metaphor for how your marketing campaign–and your career, for that matter–is built one layer at a time. Sure, there are more sophisticated ideas and business-like terms, but nothing about achieving a *Wow* has to be overly academic or even rocket science. In fact, we know of nothing more memorable than a great meal, dish, or culinary experience that invites you back time and time again to dig in and enjoy.

Food is a universal language of passion mixed with vision, and nothing in the food world is accomplished without harmony, the ingredients, and precise execution. In fact, food is on our minds more than most things! If we asked you to name some of the top chefs, your favorite dishes, or your favorite restaurants right now, like most people, you could probably rattle off a list.

Every new opportunity leads to other opportunities. And extending the comparison to lasagna, the secret to success is being mindful of how all the layers and all the ingredients blend with and complement other. When you put together enough *Wows*, you achieve a *Wow*!

This approach forms the foundation of our system of success: create a unique idea that fills a need or solves a problem, target the qualities that make it (and you) distinctive, build your brand around those qualities, and get out the word in every way possible. Now let's step back and look at the layering process. As you continue your journey to *Wow* success, keep in mind that the most successful companies–and people–in the world didn't start out being successful. They went through many ups and downs, high and lows, and faced a lot of challenges. With each success and with each failure, with each experience and with each lesson learned, they grew stronger. In this way, if we can switch metaphors for a moment, they built their success like the rings of a tree. With each ring, the tree widens and strengthens, and soon it can weather any storm.

✳ BRANDING AT THE RANCH

At Mel Zuckerman's Canyon Ranch in Tucson, Arizona, the branding has nothing to do with burning a mark on cattle. It's about an image that has been created during the past 30 years by Zuckerman, its founder, who has built Canyon Ranch into one of the most recognized and respected names in the health resort marketplace. Zuckerman created Canyon Ranch in 1979 as a place where guests dieted, exercised, and lost both weight and stress. He got the idea after spending a month in a similar place in California. He returned home with a vision for a resort where people could find their own personal empowerment relative to their health and well-being, sold his investments, and began building Canyon Ranch. He and cofounder wife Enid, who shared this dream, grew the ranch by word of month, offering low-calorie gourmet food, more luxury, and a world-class staff of professionals and leading experts in lifestyle medicine. In short, they knew their customers.

As those customers enjoyed the experience and returned home to rave about it, word spread. The brand was built through the layers we've been discussing in this book. Today, Canyon Ranch is synonymous with all healthy-lifestyle resorts. A second resort is located in Lenox, Massachusetts; there's a new hotel lifestyle resort opening in Miami Beach; and day spas continue to open in major cities with the support of CEO Jerry Cohen and President Kevin Kelly. Zuckerman, now 79 years old, continues to find ways to build and expand the brand. Companies throughout the health industry contact him in hopes of licensing deals with Canyon Ranch. Zuckerman epitomizes a number of the laws we use in this book. He had a *Wow* experience that he calls his "aha moment," built his brand and a buzz, and at an age when most of us think about retiring, he continues to stay hungry. "I consider Canyon Ranch to be one of the great business inventions of the last 25 years," says Michael Silverstein, managing director at Boston Consulting Group, in a *Newsweek* article by Daniel McGinn. We consider it a Wow with many great layers.

✴ ROBYN'S LAYERS

In an earlier chapter I talked about how I got started, working my way from stay-at-home to local shopping expert to nationally recognized consumer advocate. Another story I want to share that shows how layering works involves my daughter, Ali. I'll never forget when at the young age of 12 she wrote a book that was published entitled, *The Thank You Book for Kids*, on the value of saying "Thank you." Ali wrote to famous people throughout the country who she thought other kids would find interesting, such as Michael Eisner and the president of Harvard. She asked them who taught them to say thank you or if they teach saying thank you at Harvard, and they were so generous and wrote her back.

After the book was published, Ali gave a workshop for a Girl Scout troop, and a local newspaper wrote a story about it. A producer at CNN read about her and called to book Ali on CNN news, which was a huge publicity opportunity. When people from other shows saw her interviewed on prime time on CNN, the calls poured in asking Ali to address how parents can motivate kids to want to write thank-you notes and share in her mission to spread kindness. When the CNN host, whose name was Mark, asked how he can inspire his own children to write thank-you notes, Ali replied, "In my book I teach kids how to have fun with words. For example, take someone's name and give a compliment. Like your name, for example, Mark." And in seconds Ali came up with "MARK. . . M stands for magnificent, A stands for articulate, R stands for remarkable, and K stands for kind." Ali knew her content, gave a creative example of her ideas in action, and the publicity continues to this day. All because Ali had agreed to help a Girl Scout troop earn a thank-you badge. That one article led to others, which led to others.

Ali's experience shows how one little idea can lead to many opportunities. When you catapult a business idea, product, or any message you wish to share with the public, the first thing is that you must be authentic. You must have a dedicated interest in spreading the word, recognize that every piece of publicity is important, and have a clear picture in your mind of what you want to see happen. Visualize the type of publicity that matters. Get to know the reporter or host so that you connect on a meaningful level versus just telling your story. Layering success also comes from years of growth and learning and gaining credentials. I've always believed that little accomplishments add up to big results.

✳ RICK'S LAYERS

I graduated from college with a BFA in acting and direction and then a BS in communications. My first job after school in 1976 was at WOR radio in Manhattan producing for *The Barry Farber Show*. At the time, Barry Farber was one of the most famous talk show hosts in radio. People were calling all the time to book guests on the show, and some of them were famous people, including President Jimmy Carter. I booked them all. I was earning $125 a week, which was $92 after taxes, but I realized the power of booking guests on shows. I learned a lot. Then Mike Levine, a publicist who had started a company in 1962 called Planned TV Arts and who was always pitching his clients to me, asked me if I wanted to work for him. I did. Through Mike I learned so much, especially how much I didn't know. I was calling *Donahue* and never even knew it might not be possible to book my clients.

Three or four months after I started, I was thrown in the hot seat. Mike went in for a heart bypass operation, and I had to run the company by myself. I hired a secretary and just flew by the seat of my pants. Six months later, Mike returned, and we were doing double the business. I said, "Guess what—we're partners." We worked out a deal, and I bought into the company. Mike was my mentor, and in 18 years of partnership we never had a fight. In 1990, Mike had another bypass operation, and at that point, he retired. I bought his share of the company. At a big retirement party for Mike, I began chatting with some folks from Ruder Finn, the largest privately owned public relations firm in New York. A few years later I merged it with Ruder Finn, and the company grew from 15 employees to 55 in three years. The rest, as they say, is history.

The point of my story is that one opportunity can lead to a bigger one. Marketing campaigns and personal careers are built on connections and relationships and being willing to change. Just because you're older or more experienced doesn't mean that your way is the best way. Don't get stuck in the trap of "This is the way we've always done it." That's how companies—and people—stop growing.

Another point to my story is that it's important to treat the people you meet along the way with kindness, generosity, and respect. Building a campaign and a career is all about connections, and building connections is all about remembering that nobody forgets. If you do something to help people when they're down, they won't forget your kindness. If you do something to hurt people, they don't forget that either. The world of business—and the business of life—is all about relationships and helping people. When you are kind and generous, the universe will reward you. Your kindness and generosity will come back to help you.

Another important point to remember as you build your layers on your way to *Wow* success is to have a positive attitude. We all have emergencies and surprises and challenges thrown at us every day. The secret to your success is how you react. Stay calm and be positive. Assume there's a solution, and you'll find one. Zig Zigler is one of my heroes in life, and I keep one of his best lines in my mind: "It's your attitude not your aptitude that determines your altitude."

✳ CONNECT THE LAYERS

As you continue to put your plan into action, certain connections will seem inevitable. A newspaper article or public appearance often leads to another. Meeting someone with whom you can form an alliance can bring unforeseen resources and connections that can help you. Use this book as a type of checklist and review the laws as you move forward. Also review your business plan's timeline that we discussed in Chapter 1. We'll discuss measuring your success in more depth in Chapter 12, but always find a way to keep your eye on the big picture. That way you'll see how the layers are working. When starting a new business or launching a campaign, it's very easy to get locked into what's happening from day to day. You have deadlines and deals to make. You have this or that fire to put out. Before you know it, you can't see beyond what absolutely must be done that day. And soon enough weeks and months have passed, and you've lost sight of your overall plan. Opportunities for adding new layers and for creating profitable synergies are being missed. If you allocate a certain time every week to step back and assess your efforts, your failures and successes, you'll see new opportunities, and you'll be able to continue to work with your layers.

As author and motivational speaker Brian Tracy puts it, "You have to put in many, many, many tiny efforts that nobody sees or appreciates before you achieve anything worthwhile." Raised in a family that struggled financially, Tracy spent his twenties traveling the world, beginning his college education at the age of 30. Since then, he has built an incredibly successful career through his books and seminars on sales and marketing. His career is a study in building in layers. His following advice speaks to the heart of this law of marketing success: "I've found that luck is quite predictable. If you want more luck, take more chances. Be more active. Show up more often." Now get out there and work on those layers, build toward your goal, and get lucky. ✳

CHAPTER 12

Remember, Timing Is Everything

Strategy and timing are the Himalayas of marketing.
Everything else is the Catskills.

—Al Ries

In marketing, as in comedy, timing is everything. The world has to be ripe for your idea in order for it to have the impact you want to create. If you fill a need or desire that exists at the moment, you can achieve *Wow* success. If your idea is too late to the table, the feast will be gone. If it's too far ahead of its time, your guests will not be ready for it. As you develop your idea, pay close attention to timing.

A scene from the 1985 movie *Back to the Future* provides a perfect illustration of the importance of timing. In the movie, the main character, Marty McFly, has traveled 30 years into the past through the power of a time machine. While in the past, and through an elaborate series of events, he finds himself playing at the high school dance where his parents first fell in love in 1955. He winds up playing the song "Johnny B. Goode," a golden oldie to Marty's 1985 way of thinking, but the high school kids in the 1950s had never heard anything quite like it. The gymnasium explodes into a dervish of dancing. As the teens gyrate to the "new" beat, Marty McFly inadvertently gives birth to rock and roll. The time was right for a new sound to break through.

Near the end of the song, Marty takes a solo on the guitar, but instead of keeping with the golden-oldie style, he breaks into a heavy-metal riff circa 1985 that stops everyone, including the other musicians in the band, in their tracks. They're astonished, confused, mouths collectively agape. The timing, obviously, wasn't right for *that* new sound. It was too far ahead of the time. The kids did-n't dig it because they just didn't "get" it.

Okay, not exactly one of the most illustrious scenes in film history, but for our purposes, it's certainly one of the most illustrative. As you develop your idea, be mindful of timing. Ask yourself when is the best time to launch your product, service, or campaign. Have you targeted a market that is ready for what you have to offer? Is there anything else serving that market right now? Is some social trend creating a new need that hasn't been served?

Think of the products that have created a *Wow* success in recent years. How did they fit the time when they were made available? What need did they meet?

☀ THINK PINK

Cynthia Good had a vision. She wanted to run a business magazine for professional women, one that spoke to the obstacles women face and one that acknowledged a softer, feminine side. Women were entering the business world in increasing numbers, but no publication was speaking specifically to their needs. There was nothing like it on the market, which can be as scary as it is energizing. Were women—and men, for that matter—ready for such a leap?

Cynthia knew that *she* was ready, so along with business partner Genevieve Bos she founded a magazine and called it *PINK*. The first issue appeared on newsstands in June 2005. Readers immediately recognized the uniqueness of the approach, although not all were prepared for it. Some even wrote angry letters, objecting to the soft approach and even the magazine's name. In the markets where women were becoming consumers, particularly in sports and recreation, manufacturers had begun creating new products that took the approach known as "shrink it and pink it." Women objected, wanting products designed with their needs in mind. And here was a new magazine call-ing itself *PINK*, acknowledging the feminine side.

"We wanted to be soft and powerful at the same time," Good remembers. "Women demanded [that] it was not enough to go to work ever day without being who you really are. So we learned never to apologize for being PINK and stood our ground."

In standing their ground, they have hit a timely chord with the growing number of women in the workplace who want to blend their professional goals with their own personal style. Rather than hide their "pink" side, they could now embrace it. Good had intuited a trend that others hadn't recognized.

"Yes, we've grown, but it took time," Good recalls. "For a while, we got no PR, and then in a period of six weeks in our third year, we were featured on *Good Morning America*, CNN, [the] *New York Times*, CNBC, and *Fox and Friends*. But they called us!" Never ones to miss out on what's happening right now, *PINK* has launched PINK TV, an interactive online feature through which readers can watch instructive videos on various career topics led by national experts.

Beyond the point that timing is crucial to your success, the *PINK* story shows the importance of believing in your idea, and in your belief that the time is right, even when others don't share your vision.

✳ WHAT WOMEN WANT

Kenneth Jay Lane is considered the real thing, but his stunning jewelry is not. He built a legendary career on the premise that even fakes can be fabulous. His sought-after costume jewelry, which is sold around the world, has caught the eye of the world's most glamorous women for over four decades, including Jackie Onassis, Elizabeth Taylor, the Duchess of Windsor, and Audrey Hepburn. Moreover, his pieces are now as sought-after and collectable as precious gems, with vintage pieces selling at Christies and Sotheby's.

Lane graduated from the Rhode Island School of Design in 1954 and moved to New York for a stint in the art department at *Vogue* magazine. This experience whet his appetite for fashion, and he started with shoes. While working for

Christian Dior, he began to embellish shoes with rhinestones and play around with ideas for jewelry. His first designs sold old in minutes. Before long, his collections were being snapped up by hot boutiques and department stores across Manhattan, as well as by royalty and movie stars. He was proving that costume jewelry could be as beautiful as the "real thing" and that women were ready to wear it.

"I didn't study jewelry, and I didn't know what not to do," Lane says. "For me, it was about having an imagination and knowledge about what good jewelry looks like. Before I arrived on the scene, faux jewelry was never worn by fashionable ladies. It was used at fashion shows, but it stopped there because ladies who bought couture had their own real jewelry. As styles and the world changed, women started wearing costume jewelry, and I've personally been very fortunate. When Audrey Hepburn was filming *Breakfast at Tiffany's*, she invited me to Tiffany's to have breakfast and have coffee. In the film, she actually wore my pearl necklace, which had an elaborate clasp in the front and five strands of pearls cascading down her back. Faye Dunaway wore my jewelry in *The Thomas Crown Affair* and even insisted that I get a screen credit."

Lane's artistry came along at a time when women were ready to embrace it, and his skill and vision matched the taste of the times. As we've said throughout this chapter, timing is everything. Deliver your *Wow* when people are ready for it.

"What *Wows* me is that I reach so many people all over the world," Lane says. "I've been on QVC for 16 years, but when I see so many women on the streets and they are wearing my jewelry, it gives me great satisfaction. In business, the important thing is to really love what you do. It's when success arrives that you really have to start to work. I started out working 18 hours a day and seven days a week. From wrapping packages to doing my own bookkeeping, your work ethic is very important. Having a little splash is nice, but a little splash does not make an Olympic swimmer. Exposure is very important, but I know and study what women want. I go to museums all over the world and get inspiration from Renaissance paintings as well as great collections in Dresden, Munich, Russia, and all over the world. I attend exhibitions at the top auction houses and know what good emeralds look like. However, there's one thing I can always count on. When it comes to women, they will always want something new!"

✳ A MATTER OF LIFE AND DEATH

Dr. Henry Heimlich was a successful surgeon specializing in the chest and throat and in problems with swallowing. In the 1950s, he created a new type of operation on the esophagus. He was very interested, therefore, and very surprised to read one day in the early 1970s in the *New York Times* that choking was the sixth most common cause of accidental death.

"I had thought choking to death was a rare occurrence," he recalls. "I said this is something I should become aware of." Many people died of choking every year, though some of the deaths were initially thought to be heart attacks. A person, while eating, would pitch forward into his or her food and die. This form of death earned the nickname "café coronary."

Heimlich felt that if such deaths were so common, we were using the wrong method of trying to save the victims. Through research, he learned that the recommended method for helping a choking person was to pound him or her on the back. Further research led him to conclude that this approach actually worsened the situation.

"It drives objects tighter into the airway," he explained. "If you were able to breathe before, you're now not able to breathe. Backslapping was worse than useless. Being a chest surgeon, I knew there was enough air in the lungs [and] that if you could compress the lungs, you would get a flow of air that would push the object toward the mouth."

Through continued research and experimentation, he created a method focused on compressing air in the lungs and then pushing the air up through the windpipe, forcing the lodged object up and out of the mouth. In 1974, he published an article in a medical journal announcing his discovery. He called his method the "abdominal thrust." Not exactly a catchy name. The American Medical Association, in an article published later that year, christened the method the *Heimlich maneuver*.

Of course, in saving a life with this maneuver, timing truly is *everything*. Wait too long, and the person chokes to death. But timing also was crucial in spreading the word. The sooner people learned to use the Heimlich maneuver, the more lives would be saved.

The key, says Dr. Heimlich, was simplicity. "I spent a lot of my research time simplifying so that anyone can learn it," he says. "You have to keep it simple. Otherwise, people would keep dying. It had to be easy to learn. The simplicity was imperative."

Dr. Heimlich notes that the youngest child to save someone using his now world-famous method was a four-year-old who saved a two-year-old. Because he kept it simple, more than 30 years after the first published report, tens of millions of people a year have learned how to use the Heimlich maneuver.

As we discussed earlier in this book, you must be aware of how the layers of your plan for success work together. Keep your marketing message simple to make it easy to repeat and pass along. As others easily spread your message, it spreads faster, allowing you to take advantage of the moment. When you need to capitalize on a trend, you need to move quickly. Keep it simple, and you'll increase your speed.

The widespread use of the Heimlich maneuver did more than sell products, of course. It saved lives. Although he realized that the maneuver filled an enormous need, Dr. Heimlich admits he had no idea back in 1974 that his method, or his name, would become so famous.

"I knew it had to get out to the public or it would be useless," he said. "I didn't know it was going to be called the Heimlich maneuver, and I have to say

I had no concept of what it would become. But everyone I meet today knows the name. I knew if I could get it out, it would save lives."

✳ RAMBO MARKETING

At around the same time that Henry Heimlich was first reading about the need to help choking victims, a little-known professor of literature at the University of Iowa published his first novel, the story of a highly trained Vietnam vet suffering from posttraumatic stress disorder. In the novel, through a series of events, the vet, John Rambo, ends up battling a small-town police force in rural Kentucky.

The novel wasn't a best-seller by any stretch, but it sold well and attracted many reviews, as well as attention from Hollywood. In the 1970s, though, the theme of a Vietnam vet as a victim didn't sit well in the midst of anti-war sentiment. Script after script was submitted to studio after studio, but none wanted to touch it.

The professor, whose name is David Morrell, didn't perceive the book as pro-war. He simply saw the character as an individual, someone trained to kill who now wanted to be left alone. It was written as a thriller, not as a political statement, but the times were such that anything with a Vietnam connection was going to whip up controversy.

Professor Morrell published three more novels in the 1970s, all of which sold well enough to keep his publisher interested, but none sold so well that his literary star seemed particularly bright. Then, in 1982, the movie based on the novel about the Vietnam vet, *First Blood*, was released. Times had changed. Society had moved far enough away from the memories of the Vietnam war and the conflicts in America to see the character as a person separate from politics. The movie quickly became a megahit and launched the professor right along with it. His next books immediately hit the best-seller lists. One of them, *The Brotherhood of the Rose*, was turned into a miniseries aired right after the Super Bowl—as prime as television scheduling gets!

With the sudden, stunning success of *First Blood*, Morrell learned another valuable lesson about the importance of timing. "It was 10 years between the publication of *First Blood* and the release of the movie," Morrell recalls. "You have to think of a career as a long-term arc of time. Sometimes someone gets lucky right from the start, and for others it takes awhile. I had 10 years as a publishing writer before the Rambo phenomenon. That seasoned me. It helped me keep things in perspective."

"The key," says Morrell, "is focusing on ideas that excite you rather than merely chasing trends in hopes of getting attention. The world today turns so quickly that what's hot today is yesterday's news tomorrow. By the time a trend is in full bloom, it's usually already beginning to fade.

"I once had an editor say to me, 'Why don't you write a book like Dan Brown [author of *The Da Vinci Code*]?' I said, 'Why would I want to?' The point is that you have to be a first-rate version of yourself rather than a second-rate version of another writer."

Morrell isn't alone in being an "overnight success" who had spent years working on his ideas. He acknowledges that timing often is a matter of luck—being at the right place at the right time with the right product. But he adds that we also need to help our luck along the way.

"To a certain degree we have to make our luck," he says. "If I hadn't done *First Blood* and other books in the meantime, I couldn't have taken advantage of the luck when I became very visible. I was able to do it because I'd been working steadily."

✳ BEWARE THE BANDWAGON

David Morrell's view on writing holds true no matter what business you're in. If you foresee a developing trend, you certainly should consider ways to take advantage of your insight, but be sure that the idea you develop to fit that trend is one you're passionate about, one you believe in, one that excites you.

Also be sure you're recognizing a genuine need rather than only a trend. When the Atkins diet craze was in full bloom in 2003 and 2004, companies rushed to market their latest low-carb products. Some succeeded. Most didn't. Consumers had so many new low-carb options to choose from that there was no pressing need for more. While opening a bakery would have been a really bad idea during this trend, adding a "me too" product to a glutted market wasn't a whole lot wiser.

The list of failed products aimed at the aging baby-boomer market is equally long. Marketers salivate at the size of the demographic and try to concoct ways to reach it. The vast numbers of baby boomers hasn't exactly been a secret for the past 60 years, and so many companies have tried to appeal to them. We're not saying that you should ignore a large market, of course, but be sure that you've detected a real need within that market.

☀ BE READY FOR SUCCESS—ROBYN

Timing is everything, and you must plan for success in order to achieve it. Forget overnight successes. Sure, it'd be a perfect world if that's all it took, but we agree that you have to build that field of dreams. It's the only way you'll be ready when opportunities knock or you spot one worth pursuing. I learned early in my career as a how-to expert and consumer advocate on television to plan months ahead of time, anticipating themes, topics of extreme interest, and upcoming holidays.

Year after year, I research, test, forecast, and consume myself with finding the most innovative gifts and products that have a *Wow* in them. I'll never forget one e-mail that arrived on my screen over five years ago, and it was the invitation of a lifetime.

It was the holiday season, and I was sitting at my computer answering questions from writers and media all over the country who call and count on me during the holidays for innovative gift-giving ideas. Though an everyday occurrence, I'm ready to address their calls, which are often time-sensitive. So it wasn't unusual that I received an e-mail inquiring about my gift-giving knowledge. When I looked at who the media query was from, to my astonishment, it was a producer at *The Today Show*. You could have knocked me over, but I knew that I was up to the challenge. Holy *Wow*, I thought! At that very minute I recall taking a deep breath, screaming in my mind "Yes!" and feeling much like I assume Rocky felt as he made his way into the ring for his big match.

I immediately picked up the telephone and called the producer. I had worked for over 20 years, day in and day out, 12 months a year reporting on gifts and products and had been on national shows, but getting an invitation from a producer at *The Today Show* was one of my most memorable and exciting moments in time.

The producer introduced herself, replied she had enjoyed and used ideas from my books for a few years, and then preinterviewed me at length about the topic. Before I knew it, I was booked! A week later I was on a plane headed to appear on *The Today Show*. Years later, and with multiple appearances to date, I still feel so grateful for each appearance. My goal continues as I am always prepared because timing is everything, I've never taken any of my appearances locally or nationally for granted. My best advice? Be ready, be overprepared, and always, always deliver more than anyone expects. Plus, always say thank you. None of us rises to the top without someone helping or believing in us, and I remain deeply grateful to my first producer ever and all the producers, hosts, and talent who have made my dreams possible through the years.

☀ WHAT ARE YOU READY TO DO?

Each of us has a *Wow*, so what are you prepared to do? Are you ready for more customers? Are you prepared to unveil a new concept? Are you chomping at the bit with an invention and pursuing the patent or trademark on an idea? And have you considered the moment in time when you will share this with the world? Who will appreciate your information or business the most? Do they have time and energy to listen? Yes, timing is everything, but we also know that everything is everything, so keep your eye on the dial. Keep your focus on the target, and be ready for success and be ready with all *i*s dotted and *t*s crossed when it's time to launch. ✳

CHAPTER 13

Spread the Word

All publicity is good, except an obituary notice.

—Brendan Behan

Your marketing campaign is like calling everyone to the table for a feast that you've worked long and hard to prepare. You must make your call loud and clear and rely on the people nearby to spread the word throughout the house: dinner is served. In short, you build word of mouth. And when those guests have been served—and have given their lip-smacking raves of delight—you rely on them to spread the word about the meal.

Let's face it, when someone raves about a product, an idea, a movie, a restaurant, a service, or a book, you want to know more about it. You go. You show up. You try it yourself. Word of mouth is one of the most powerful marketing tools available to us. As marketers, we need to get people talking because those people can be far more persuasive (and far less expensive) than any catchphrase or advertisement we can create.

Why? Because in today's world of media saturation, consumers hear far more messages than they can absorb. They filter out most of those messages, and they tend to be cynical about those that do break through the roar. They assume that the claim is, at best, exaggerated and, at worst, completely false. We all do it. We see a commercial on television or an ad in a magazine, and we try to assess whether or not to believe it. A recent report on consumer receptivity by trend watchers Yankelovich Partners, Inc., shows that 93 percent of customers don't believe the marketing messages they hear and see. Most of the time, we barely hear the message at all, and when we do, we quickly forget it.

But if our neighbor or office colleague or family member comes to us raving about something, we are much more likely to hear the message in a positive way. We're much more willing to believe.

This is one reason why marketers use testimonials—from person-on-the-street interviews to endorsements on the backs of books. We want to get people talking in positive ways about our subject, and we want that talk to trigger even more talk. Before you know it, people are saying, "I've heard about that. I heard it's great!" Think of how many highly touted movies have been launched through huge marketing budgets only to flop after the first few weeks. The culprit: word of mouth. People saw it, didn't like it, and told their family and friends. Of course, the reverse also occurs. A small art-house film can play for months as word spreads that it's a gem.

In the Afterword to the updated edition of *The Tipping Point*, Malcolm Gladwell writes, "What is now obvious to me—but wasn't at the time I wrote *The Tipping Point*—is that we are about to enter the age of word of mouth."

☀ THE ICING ON THE CAKE

Recently, Robyn brought a sampling of over-the-top, truly amazing cakes to her radio station for her monthly *Giftionary* gift-giving show and set up a sampling in the studio kitchen. Within seconds, the radio station staff gravitated to the cakes, devoured them, and while the raving *Wows* were flying in the room, but the best compliment of all was, "These cakes are not just *Wow*, they are Way *Wow*!"

Everyone talked about the cakes for days, and the word spread like wildfire. They have since referred endless customers to these world-class cakes. Each person has his or her favorite, but the memorable taste of those decadent cakes was etched in each person's mind.

The same *Wow* applied to cookies that Robyn discovered in her gift research baked by HeidisHeavenlyCookies.com, a sinfully delicious cookie company owned by Heidi Nel. Heidi's decadent cookies have since been repeatedly featured in the national media and fans become voluntary cookie ambassadors spreading their gourmet gratitude for Heidi. In fact, Heidi's Toffee Chocolate Chip cookie causes such a sensation every time Robyn features it along with her newest cookies in Atlanta, that her *Giftionary* radio show crew on Star 94 with Cindy and Ray often tease her not to come back unless she brings Heidi's heavenly cookies.

When something or someone is outstanding, tempts our taste buds, evokes an emotion, or peeks our curiosity, we talk about it. It's not rocket science, and it's certainly not surprising. In fact, it can be surprisingly simple. Give the consumer something to talk about. Spreading the word is simply spreading a small story that we personalize and call our own. It's what makes great cocktail party conversation, but in big business, it's what makes sales and products catapult. It provokes attention and raises the interest of purchasers, supporters, and advocates for your product, service, or message and even you!

☀ BUILDING A BUZZ

A few years ago, Proctor & Gamble (P&G) took the power of word of mouth to a new level by starting a marketing agency called Tremor, through which it hires popular teens to talk about P&G products to their friends and families. Other corporations, such as Coca-Cola and America Online, have signed up as clients in the hope of using these "stealth marketers" to grab more of the teen market.

Some people debate the ethics of such a drastic approach, but the point is that marketers understand the power of word of mouth. In your marketing efforts, be sure to keep that power in mind. Get your message to as many people as possible, and make your message so powerful that those people will eagerly spread the word for you. Make a list of all the means you have for spreading the word and sparking word of mouth.

Willy Spizman, CEO of The Spizman Agency, (www.spizmanagency.com) a public relations firm in Atlanta, Georgia, is Robyn's husband and a true expert at spreading the word, helping experts and authors reach national success. He sheds light for us on ways to do it:

"It's important to understand your connectors and how a message is spread," he says. "The media is the obvious source used to spread a message, but it's a matter of degrees of separation, and the goal is to take the six degrees and reduce it. It's a who-knows-who-knows-who approach. A viral campaign enlisting foot soldiers, people who carry your message from person to person, place to place, also proves to be an effective method. It's similar to the connect-the-dots game. Every dot counts. Demographics also matter in the verbal transport of the message. People who are vested in you, your message, product, or service, will add passion and a persuasive point of view. Expert positioning, turning authors into authorities and people into personalities so they are viewed as a credible resource with a take-home message, will also help spread your message. If you first provide a benefit that maximizes a message, then sales will follow. Give those connectors—people, the media, experts, and authors—something to spread, a story they can make their own, something to talk about, and the message will travel at lightning speed."

We spread the word for numerous reasons. We are curious. We are enthusiastic about something. We dislike or disapprove of and wish to prevent someone else from trying something out. We are excited. We want to inform others. Think about the last time you found yourself spreading the word on someone else's idea, product, or service. Ask yourself why you were compelled to do it. Your answer will guide your own efforts at spreading the word.

☀ HEARD IT THROUGH THE PIPELINE

Stedman Graham—businessman, speaker, and author of ten books, including *Build Your Own Life Brand*—offers sparkling insight into both layering and word of mouth:

"You don't reach millions all at once," he says. "You must layer the process. It's about bringing people into your core base who want to come, but you have to create pipelines for them. Pipelines are simply ways they can enter. You have to find where your audience is and then create paths for them to reach you. For example, I reach the public through speeches, seminars, workshops, trade shows, a Web site, and interviews. You have to create a connection to the marketplace and make it easy for them to find and come to you, and they will come looking for you. Everyone wants to go through the media and thinks that's the only way to get to the public and that it's all about the sizzle. Sizzle fizzles. Instant gratification is not the way to get to people, since if it sizzles out, there's nothing left. You have to get through to the culture of the society, and you have to get through with a strong connection. If you want to find the target market of that culture, you have to organize around that segment of the population and go where they go. Go where they value. You must focus around the marketplace and build mind share."

✳ THE LOVE YOU MAKE

To spark interest in and buzz about your idea, tell everyone you know about it. Begin to build those "pipelines," which can flow both ways—bringing an audience of people to your idea as well as a network of people who can help you to develop, refine, and advance your idea. You never know who can help or who will know someone who knows someone who knows someone who holds the key to your success—or at least can add an important layer to your feast.

In fact, don't wait until you're ready to launch your marketing effort before you begin building your pipelines. Start now. A successful marketer needs to have a network of people to call on—contacts in various fields who can offer expertise and assistance—so begin building your network. Make a conscious effort to get to know people and their interests, concerns, and backgrounds. The highest praise marketers can receive is when people say, "You know everybody."

You might wonder, however, how you use your network when you're ready to build your buzz. The question arises, How do I get them to lend a hand?

The answer: by lending *them* a hand.

When you're willing to go out of your way to help people, particularly when they are having a tough time, they remember. They are much more willing to help you when you need them. By being open to people, by listening to them and making them feel valued, you build your network, which is a very handy thing to have when you're trying to build a buzz. It's like the Beatles told us many years ago: "The love you take is equal to the love you make."

So get out there and make some love.

Gary and Diane Heavin built their business in just that way and stayed ahead of the curve. In 1992, their vision was to create a place for women, 35 and up to get physically fit. Gary's mom was obese and had died of complications from diabetes that could have been prevented. While he attended medical school in the early seventies, Gary ran out of money and had to drop out. Along with his wife, he initiated the vision of a fitness facility for every woman's budget and opened the first Curves in Harlingen, S. Texas to help the women in their local community. Like wildfire, the Curves name spread and they opened the second one a few years later. The Heavins wanted the passion of dedicated owners, so they developed the Curves franchise.

Even without a national advertising campaign until 2003, there were already 6,000 Curves with almost three million members worldwide. From zero to 6,000 clubs the concept spread in lightening speed. Most of the owners are former members and 90 percent are women. It was simple. Women tried it. Women loved it. Women bought it. Now, Curves is the fastest growing franchise in history and the largest fitness company with over 10,000 locations and four million members in every state in the U.S. and in 58 countries including Australia, Israel, and Ireland. Curves spreads the love by being committed to strengthening women's minds, spirits, and bodies. They continue to nourish souls by being committed to inspiring their franchises that have collected over 80 million pounds of food to help local community food banks.

※ TIP THE BABYSITTER

New Yorker Karen Quinn put word of mouth to work at the highest level. She registered her dreams with everyone she knew. As a former counselor at a private school, where she helped parents get their preschoolers into the Ivy Leagues even before they were born, she believed that she could turn her experience into a blockbuster novel. When she sat down to write *The Ivy Chronicles*, her objective was to write a best-seller. Nothing less.

Quinn's goal was ridiculous for a lot of reasons. First, she'd never written anything before. Second, all the books tell you not to write for money or you'll be sorely disappointed. Third, it was a long shot that she'd find an agent or a publisher. But she had a story she wanted to tell, and she wanted to write a book that she'd like to read. Every chapter was written with this in mind. Unfortunately, she couldn't afford to write as a hobby. She had bills to pay and needed to sell her work.

When Quinn completed the first draft, she mentioned it to her babysitter, Bev, who recalled that years before she had taken care of a boy who played with a boy whose mother worked in the publishing field. When Bev offered to call the woman, Quinn didn't believe the contact was likely to help. However, as it turned out, Bev's contact was an agent—a famous, successful agent. As a favor to Bev, the agent agreed to read the manuscript. Amazingly enough, she loved it and offered to represent it.

Weeks later, Quinn's husband, Mark, remembered that he had met a woman at a track and field meet who worked in publishing. Although he didn't know her well, he called her and told her about Quinn's book. The woman turned out to be a high-ranking editor, whose list of successful books included *The Devil Wears Prada*, by Lauren Weisberger, a blockbuster. She asked to read

Quinn's manuscript and made the first bid on it. A hot bidding war ensued, and Quinn landed a big contract.

But the story gets juicier. Quinn's agent was able to get actor Catherine Zeta-Jones to read the novel, and the big star wanted to star in a movie based on the novel. The agent got Jerry Weintraub on board to produce the film, and Warner Brothers bought the film rights.

Quinn, who could have been satisfied with all of these events, went on to tell everyone she knew and met about her new book. She invested her own word of mouth and enlisted friends and family to tell everyone they knew about the book and to suggest they buy it. She provided an e-mail letter template that anyone could send and even turned her friends-and-family promotion into a contest with a prize for the person who delivered the biggest results.

Then she compiled her own database of targeted readers, and the publisher sent them a postcard about the book. She studied public relations in order to pitch herself for TV and radio shows and for newspaper and magazine articles.

"I asked everyone I knew if they knew people in media and if they would help me get to them," Quinn said. Lo and behold, her hairdresser introduced her to a producer on *The View*, and she got on that show. She spoke in public as often as she could so that people would hear about her book. "My publisher published minibooks of the first chapters of my book and sent them to gynecologists' offices, pediatricians' offices, orthodontists' offices, any place my target audience might be," she said.

Quinn learned not to scale back her dream just because it seemed impossible to accomplish. She also learned to tell everyone she knew what she was doing, and her motto became, "You never know who will help you." Her biggest helpers were her babysitter, her husband's friend from the track meet, and hairdressers. She never expected them to have such an impact on her success.

✳ BE CONTAGIOUS

To ignite a buzz about your product, you need to get people talking. To do that, you need to give them something to say. In his book, *Buzzmarketing*, Mark Hughes astutely advises, "Give people a great story to tell." Let them know the story of your product or service. How did it get started? What circumstances led to its creation? Or give them a story about an experience you've had trying to market your idea. Make it funny or surprising, a story people are going to want to tell others. Think about the stories you tell your friends, the e-mails you forward, and the links you send. Examine them to infer what qualities these pieces share, and then find a way to develop a story that has those same qualities.

Marketers sometimes bemoan the difficulty in making a splash in today's marketplace owing to the recent advances in technology that flood the consumer with messages. Instead, use that technology to your advantage by creating a message that people can pass on more easily than ever before.

Viral marketing is a powerful tool for spreading the word. Make your message strong enough that people will want to pass it on. And make it *easy* to pass along. The most famous recent example of viral marketing success is Hotmail, the e-mail service provider started in July of 1996. In less than three years, Hotmail reached 30 million members. The company did it by using members to get members. Signing up was easy, and it was even easier to pass along the registration link to friends and family. That kind of growth goes beyond viral—it was an epidemic.

With this success in mind, many marketers have used Internet technology as the basis for viral campaigns. In recent years, You Tube has been the most popular medium. The video-sharing site was created in February 2005 and acquired by Google in October 2006 for an estimated $1.65 billion in Google stock. The phenomenal growth and popularity of You Tube has drawn marketers like bees to honey. Company after company has posted funny commercials, some too spicy for prime-time network television. The hope is that the commercials are so entertaining—funny, moving, informative, and unique—that people will e-mail them to their friends, thus spreading the word.

"In the online video world, anyone can create a video now," says Ken McArthur, author of *Impact: How to Get Noticed, Motivate Millions, and Make a Difference in a Noisy World*. "The tools are out there to produce something of pretty decent quality. To stand out in that group, you have to create something with quality. A lot of people, when they start putting up You Tube videos, they'll put up an expert talking about something as opposed to showing how it happened in real life or telling a story."

As an example, McArthur recalls the story of Juan Mann, an Australian man who, while down on his luck personally and professionally, began a campaign to give away "free hugs" by holding up a sign in a shopping mall announcing his rather strange offer. For a while, nobody stopped. Then, according to Juan's Web site, freehugscampaign.org, "The first person who stopped, tapped me on the shoulder, and told me how her dog had just died that morning. How that morning had been the one-year anniversary of her only daughter dying in a car accident. How what she needed now, when she felt most alone in the world, was a hug. I got down on one knee, we put our arms around each other, and when we parted, she was smiling."

After that first hug, Juan started showing up in malls on a regular basis to offer free hugs. Eventually, a friend taped him doing it, set the videotape to music, and posted it on You Tube in September 2006. By December, the tape had received 17 million views.

"They put it up on You Tube on a Friday night," McArthur recalls. "By Sunday, it had a quarter of a million views. *Good Morning America* broadcast it, [and] he went on *Oprah*. The campaign started spreading all over the world."

"The key," McArthur adds, "is creating a message that connects with an audience so deeply that they're compelled to pass it along. There were reasons why these guys had impact while others don't. They engaged the emotions. We live in a disconnected society. People who are by themselves want to feel connected. When you see the video, you see him walking through the mall, and it's a lonely thing."

Most of all, remember the key ingredient to building a buzz through word of mouth—Be positive. Believe with all your heart in what you're doing. You'll find that your enthusiasm is contagious. It will inspire others to help you because they will catch your fever of excitement about what you're doing. They'll want to be part of the campaign because it's exciting to be near such passion and enthusiasm.

Before she finished writing *The Ivy Chronicles*, Karen Quinn believed that it would be published and that it would be a hit. Her positive energy attracted positive people into her life, and those people helped her. If you're not thrilled by what you're marketing, it will be tough to thrill others. It won't happen. But when you are truly pleased with your creation, others will share your enthusiasm. Invite them to dinner with confidence, and get ready to hear them talking about it. And whatever you do, keep talking about it too. ✳

CHAPTER 14

Measure Your Results

*It is only the farmer who faithfully plants seeds in the
Spring who reaps a harvest in the Autumn.*

— **B. C. Forbes**

So how's it going? We're not just making idle chitchat. We mean really
and seriously, how well are you doing so far on your journey to *Wow*
success? Knowing the answer to this question in clear, specific terms is
another important step along the way. Back in Chapter 1 you made a list of
your goals for your idea, product, service, company, career, or whatever
you're undertaking right now. We also suggested that you make a timeline of
interim metrics—where you want to be in three months, a year, and so on—or
to list all the goals you want to achieve.

Keep those lists handy, and check them frequently. As we've said before,
it's easy to lose sight of the big picture when you're focused on all the day-to-
day challenges that confront you. We're not saying that you have to have a
graph with key performance indicators outlined in geometric patterns, but it's
important to be able to step back and assess your progress. There's an old saying in business: "If you can't measure it, you can't manage it." You have to set
goals and be able to see how you're doing on your way to reaching them.

☀ IN GOD WE TRUST

All others must bring data. This is one of the primary laws of life at Eureka
Ranch, run by marketing and business creativity guru Doug Hall. In his best-
selling books, *Jump Start Your Business Brain* and *Jump Start Your Marketing*

Brain, Hall places a lot of emphasis on the need for testing and measuring an idea—from the early stages throughout the process of marketing and selling. We asked him why it's so important.

"We've got a situation right now where only around 5 percent of marketing campaigns have any real impact on attracting business," he says. "It's because the marketing efforts tend not to be very disciplined. Everybody gives lip service to it, but if they actually did the testing and measuring, they'd realize how many failures they've had."

The culprit?

"There's a myth out there that marketing is an art not a science," he says. "That's why marketing officers have the shortest lifespan of any others in a typical business. Their lifespan is usually around 18 months. A headhunter once told me it's because they overpromise. They aren't willing to test and learn. A scientific method is something marketing people haven't learned. Every other area of business continues to improve except marketing."

When you've come up with an idea, says Hall, it's important to test it early in the process and to use the results to make improvements—to the product or the message or whatever you're trying to do.

"The key is to fail fast, fail cheap. It never works the first time. You have to do it again. It's a matter of continuous improvement. Big companies might do one big test market, but smart entrepreneurs do lots of little tests. Write a simple questionnaire. Go out every day and show it to 50 people. We do tests at fairs and malls at happy hours, wherever. You want answers to two basic questions—purchase intent and how new and different it is. Measure your results and use that data to make improvements."

In terms of testing and measuring, Hall suggests a game of king of the hill. "Take whatever the best product is in your category, and test yours against it," he says. "Then measure the results. It doesn't have to be complicated. An Excel spreadsheet can do the basic stuff. It's not that hard. Numbers are your friend."

☀ THE FUTURE'S SO BRIGHT

Joe Sugarman, CEO of BluBlocker Corporation, has been called a "mail-order maverick" by the *New York Times*, "one of the country's greatest copywriters" by *Bottom Line/Personal Newsletter*, and "one of the most successful direct-marketing gurus of all time" by *Success Magazine*. In 1979, Sugarman was selected as the "Direct Marketing Man of the Year," and in 1991, he was given the Maxwell Sackheim Award for his career contributions to direct marketing. In short, he's a guy who knows how to sell with his words. Since 1986, those highly crafted words have sold more than 20 million pairs of his extraordinary BluBlocker sunglasses, but he always measures his success, rather than just assuming that the ads and other direct-marketing efforts will draw the customers he seeks.

"When we promoted the brand, we took out ads in every magazine we'd ever advertised in," Sugarman recalls. "The sunglasses were so successful in every magazine. We measured all the results from our national campaign, and every ad pulled a nice response. We invested a million dollars in print ads and sold about 100,000 pairs. We then looked to infomercials. I saw that as an opportunity, and then we sold 100,000 pairs a month, and we ultimately were shipping about 300,000 pairs a month."

By measuring the success of the initial ads and continuing to hone the message based on the results, Sugarman created a world-class hit. He made sure that the message focused on showing how his sunglasses were different—and better—in a crowded, competitive market category.

Echoing Doug Hall's advice about the importance of testing, Sugarman says, "If you have a product, don't judge if it's a good seller before testing it. You must do a test run. You can show it to your relatives, but don't believe what they have to say. They tell you what you want to hear. Even focus groups will tell you what they think, but the true test is a person's hard-earned money for your product. Without that test, you have nothing. You might think with all the experience I have I can tell you if a product will succeed, but I have been so fooled by products that were huge and I thought they would bomb—and also by bombs that I thought would be huge."

In short, it pays to test your ideas and measure the results. When you're convinced that you have a winner, get it out there and continue to measure your progress and results.

✳ LARGER GOALS

We all want our ideas to pay off financially, but a true success should be measured not just in dollars. A great idea makes life better for the people around you and the people who benefit as consumers. This type of success can't be measured in a profit-and-loss statement. It doesn't show up on the bottom line. But touching people's lives, helping them through what you have to offer, is a true measure of success.

Mark Victor Hansen and his partner, Jack Canfield, have achieved spectacular success with their *Chicken Soup* series. *Chicken Soup* is surely one of the most popular brands in the publishing world today with many best-sellers and millions of copies sold. But Hansen feels that the lives that have been nurtured and comforted by the series are more important than the money that's been made and that making a real contribution to the world is a measure of success that cannot be quantified. He told us the story of one reader whose life was saved:

"We had a lovely lady who came to our seminar," he explains. "She was pregnant and feeling unloved. She was in Cincinnati, Ohio, and she was going to kill herself. Freezing, contemplating suicide, she goes into a library and finds a *Chicken Soup* book, and she finds inspiration in the story titled, 'Puppies for Sale.' She reads it, and for whatever reason, it touched her so deeply that she decided to live, have the baby, clean up her act, and finish her education. And she did that during the past seven years. She's now married and has two more kids. She started soup kitchens, and she feeds 10,000 people a month.

"Fifteen years ago I couldn't have predicted someone would have that kind of response. Now she attends our seminars, and she ultimately wants to teach all women they can survive. When people heard her story when we brought her up on stage at a seminar, there wasn't a dry eye in the house. That's a *Wow*."

Results like these cannot be measured mathematically, but they certainly can provide evidence of your success. Hansen and Canfield know that their idea has had an enormous impact on many lives.

"The size of your thinking determines the sizes of your results," Hansen adds. "Little thinking gets little results, and I'd like everyone to find their *Wow*. If all of us used our full potential, then all the problems in the universe would get solved. It would be electric. There's time, resources, money, and space for everyone to find their *Wow*." *

CHAPTER 15

Stay Hungry

I think we're having fun. I think our customers really like
our products. And we're always trying to do better.

—Steve Jobs

Okay, for this law, you might be thinking, "If only I were in a position
to fret about the fear of resting on my laurels. If only I were in jeopardy of losing my edge owing to all my fabulous success."

This is understandable. Sometimes resting on our laurels can seem like
the least of our worries. Who has so many laurels to spare that they can spend
time resting on them? But the fact is that the first blush of success can be a
dangerous time in the life of your marketing campaign. It's human nature to
want to relish the success you've achieved. When times aren't quite so desperate, when the need to succeed isn't quite so urgent, it's easy to lose sight of
the larger goals. It's easy to become less observant of opportunities and easy
to forget the hard work and the innovation that sparked the success. Instead,
we expect things to be easier.

Success breeds success, no doubt, and as you begin to achieve your goals,
you'll find that the momentum you've managed to create takes on a force of its
own. But realize that momentum alone won't get you to the level of success
you set out to achieve. Momentum has a way of lessening—even reversing—if
you don't continue to feed it. So don't lose your edge. Don't become so satisfied with what you've accomplished that you lose sight of your larger goals.
Keep your vision of *Wow* success clear in mind, and keep striving.

☀ FROM LAUNDRY TO LUXURY

In 1948, Bill Ruder and David Finn were 27 years old when they started their public relations firm. They had so little money that they set up shop in a small laundry storage area in Manhattan's Lombardy Hotel, a space given to them in exchange for agreeing to publicize the hotel's new restaurant. The tiny room with a single, small window was only big enough for a single desk, which they shared, each sitting on one side of it. From those humble beginnings, however, the pair set the world on its ear with some of the most creative publicity ideas ever seen.

"After the first year we began to realize that we had a great idea," Bill Ruder recalls. "I would do the new business, and David would run the operations of the company. I loved the idea of convincing people that I had ideas that were useful to them. We invented the concept of the field network. We put together men and women in the 30 or so key cities of the country who were in the publicity business. At that point there were three radio networks, no TV. We asked them who was the best publicist in town." In this way they built a network of associates who, when a campaign hit their town, would be the point person. Ruder and Finn would create imaginative campaigns that attracted attention to their clients. One campaign Ruder fondly recalls was for a new detergent product. "On Lincoln's Birthday, Boy Scout troops in the key cities washed the local monument to Honest Abe with the detergent, a stunt that received no end of attention in newspapers and on radio stations. We were then working for half the top Fortune 100 consumer products companies."

"Before you knew it we were growing as a regular public relations firm," Ruder says. "People would say, 'Can you do this,' and our answer was always, 'Yes.' Even when we didn't know how we would do it, we always learned."

Within 10 years, Ruder-Finn was the largest public relations firm in the country. Besides huge commercial clients such as Lever Brothers and Union Carbide, the firm soon gathered onto its list a galaxy of entertainment stars, including Perry Como, Dinah Shore, Frankie Laine, the Mills Brothers, Jack

Lemmon, and Rosalind Russell. In 1960, President John Kennedy named Ruder his assistant secretary of commerce. Although it sounds like a scene from an old movie, that's the way it happened.

Bill Ruder, now 86, is retired, although the company he helped build remains very much a presence in the world of public relations. And he remains hungry. He still does pro bono work for select clients, using the same strategies that led to his astounding success. He "stays hungry" by remaining committed to the philosophy he developed many years ago.

"It works on several different levels," he explains. "First, I love my work. Second, I love the individual challenges, one by one. It's like playing baseball—you want to win this game, and then you want to win the next game. There is also a more philosophical level. The work that we do is committed to minimizing conflict, and it helps make a difference in the world for the better. I don't mean we can change the world, but the work we do can help make the world an infinitesimally better place."

To that end, he continues to ply his skills for worthy causes. His daughter suffers from multiple sclerosis (MS), and Ruder gives considerable time and effort and a whole lot of marketing savvy to help raise money and awareness for MS.

"I do it the same way I always did it," he says. "We've raised huge amounts of money for them. That's the challenge I set up for myself."

Setting up challenges for himself is a useful strategy for keeping himself in the game, he says, even after 60 years. When you're feeling a bit stale or stagnant, give yourself a new challenge. Apply the skills you've acquired and the confidence you've gained from your success. Take on the new challenge, and feel the gusto.

☀ INSATIABLE

Deborah Fine oversees a village. NBC Universal's iVillage, that is—as it's president. This former Conde Nast publishing executive and CEO of Victoria

Secret's PINK brand now heads the leading online destination for women. She oversees 294 employees and welcomes 16 million unique visitors per month. It's all in a day's work for this self-motivated working mom.

Prior to her tenure at the lingerie giant, she served as the founder and president of Avon Future, where she helped launch Mark, the company's global cosmetics and accessories brand. Before her career in marketing, Fine was a long-time media executive, including stints as the vice president and publisher of Conde Nast's *Glamour* magazine and publisher of *Brides* magazine. During her time at *Brides*, Fine helped launch theweddingchannel.com. In 2001, when Fine interviewed for her job at Avon, she met Andrea Jung, Avon's chairman and CEO. Although Fine was entertaining many job offers, she stopped Jung eight minutes into the interview and said, "I hope this isn't too bold, but I don't care what I have to do here, I'll clean floors if needed." That was on a Monday. By Friday, Jung had created a job.

Fine has always been hungry for success. She adds, "I am insatiable, and I have an insatiable desire to win. I've lead four businesses with extreme profits, and my goal is to win and win big. I feel I am very fortunate to find myself in the twenty-fifth year of my career and working with many amazing people."

Those people no doubt continue to be amazed by Deborah Fine.

"In terms of my drive, this story is very telling," she says. "When I became publisher of *Brides* magazine, we earned the first Guinness record for the world's largest consumer magazine ever published. My staff gave me an embroidered pillow that says 'Never satisfied.' That clearly showed [that] no matter what we accomplish, there's more to achieve, and winning feels good. That motivation drives me, and whether you are a struggling entrepreneur, seasoned executive, or CEO looking for the next gig, it comes down to passion. If you don't innately believe in something passionately—the people you work with or the product you are representing or the service you are offering—I don't know how you get there. You must innately and viscerally believe in what you are doing."

Despite her "insatiable desire to win," Fine has found even more motivation to succeed from her 10-year-old son, Jake, who three years ago was diagnosed with juvenile diabetes.

"I've watched him give himself 10 shots a day, close to 4,000 shots a year, and be brave," she says. "Of all the life lessons I've learned, the ones I've learned from watching my son have been the most life-altering. My husband and our other son, Daniel, all live by the rule that 'failure is not an option.' There was no choice but to learn about diabetes, the daily management, and the emergency procedures. I can no longer doubt myself. If I do, I'm reminded that if my *kid* can conquer this, I can conquer *anything*. When my son looks at me, he looks at me to solve diabetes, and we must do everything we can to accomplish that in this lifetime. We even have a fundraising team called Brotherly Love and have raised over $300,000. One dollar at a time. You have to be hungry to live a life that makes a difference. We didn't sign up for this, but you sign up for and deal with the one you get and do the best you can to create new possibilities."

✳ WHAT'S YOUR WHY?

Throughout most of this book we've been focused on the question, "Where's your *Wow*?" To help you stay hungry and achieve your *Wow* success, let's ask a new question: "What's your *Why*?"

We learned this question from Willie Jolley, an award-winning speaker and singer, best-selling author, and media personality. He told us that he asks his audiences this question to help them find their true focus—and keep it.

"Why did you do it in the first place?" Willie asks. "Your whys have to be so strong. Is it just to make money? If so, when you make the money, what's your incentive? Is your why big enough to keep you going? Maybe your why is that you grew up in poverty. Or your why, which is my why, is that I really believe there's a need to inspire people. It has to be something that's ongoing."

Before launching his career as a motivational speaker, singer, and author, Jolley worked in the Washington, DC, school system and became frustrated by the bureaucratic obstacles and deception he faced. He told himself that he would find a new way to achieve his goal of inspiring people and never again live as he was living then. He endured the anxiety of starting a new business, wondering, at times, how he would even "keep the lights on," but through his determination, he built a hugely successful career. Despite that success, he remains committed to his larger goals.

"Your dream should be so big that you can't achieve it in your lifetime," he says. "That way you're always pursuing that goal. You keep working on it. I encourage people to have big whys. The bigger the why, the more you can stay focused. Focus on your rewards for achieving the goal. People are motivated by inspiration or desperation. They're trying to achieve something or are trying to avoid a pain. If you don't have those motivators, you'll stop pushing. You should be motivated by the things you love or the things you hate. Personally, I hate mediocrity."

Holding tightly to that conviction, Jolley speaks to companies and organizations across the country. In the fall of 2006, for example, he spoke to workers at Ford Motor Company in a number of cities. "Ford was struggling to reorganize," he says. "They'd been so big for so long, it was hard to get them going. Workers were saying, 'We've worked here for a long time and have nice cars and houses, [so] we don't have to work as hard.' They weren't moving on an initiative the president had offered. I started going to Ford plants around the country for a month, talking to people about why it's important to get reenergized. They hadn't had a profitable quarter in six quarters."

After Jolly spread his message about having big goals, the company rebounded and posted its first profitable quarter in nearly two years. Apparently, the workers had found a big enough why to renew their commitment to excellence.

So if you're starting to stagnate or just feel that you've lost a bit of the passion that fueled your early efforts, go back and recall the reasons you decided to launch your journey to *Wow*. ✳

CHAPTER 16

Put People First

People are definitely a company's greatest asset. It doesn't make any difference whether the product is cars or cosmetics. A company is only as good as the people it keeps.

—Mary Kay Ash

As you find your way to the *Wow* success you envisioned at the start of your journey, you will enjoy the rewards of your ingenuity, discipline, and hard work. The true key to your success, however, will be the passion you bring to the effort. The material gain is only one way of measuring the success; it's not success itself. You have to love what you do and feel like you're making a difference. Television star Charlie Gibson, in a farewell to legendary movie critic Joel Siegel, who died from colon cancer, said, "Joel didn't like to review plays because if he gave a bad review, the play could close down, and people would lose their jobs, and that would hurt people, but he loved reviewing movies, since people would still go and already have paid."

The road to *Wow* is full of people whose lives you touch, and as you look back, the people will be what truly matters.

✸ PEOPLE MATTER MOST

Tim Sanders is the best-selling author of *Love Is the Killer App* and an avid lecturer and former executive at Yahoo! An advocate for good values, he passionately believes that people who share generously can achieve professional success. "What I've learned is that the next big thing in business is people. Those of us who use love as a point of differentiation in business will separate ourselves from our competitors. For example, the main driver for people at work is how you are treated as a person, which is the emotional compensation plan. Along with your paycheck, you take home some sense of self-worth which is even more important and love is the killer app which makes you distinctive and sets you apart.

"Love is the promotion of other people's growth. When you mentor someone, you show love to them by helping them grow through knowledge. This is good business. For personal wealth building, the law of attraction is fine, but for business life, the law of reciprocity is far more important. People reciprocate more often than not. The norm of reciprocity works nine times out of ten. Let's say I network with ten people and then they reciprocate. They feel a sense of connection where they want to out give me, which is a human tendency.

"You need to be selective, though. Nice, smart people succeed. Not just nice, but nice and smart. People are most likely to reciprocate if you have faith in them, not because you expect them to. Put people first because they are the only entity that really generates value in the world."

✴ A MATTER OF PRINCIPAL

For 11 years, Dennis Haskins played the role of Mr. Belding, the principal of Bayside High School, on *Saved by the Bell*, one of the most successful sitcoms in television history. Millions of young people growing up between 1989 and 2000 know him as that beloved principal. Becoming a pop culture icon for a generation would seem to be a definition of *Wow* success, but Haskins feels that the truer measure of success is the joy his show brought to the legions of kids who eagerly watched and who now remember it so fondly.

"Some people think being identified closely with a role for a long period of time holds them back, and afterward they turn away from it. Sometimes it does. But it is what it is. To turn away negates a lot of love that is out there from a generation of young people, now growing up, who were, and are, devoted to what we did. I'm not going to rain on their affection. I embrace it while striving to continue to act in different movies and TV shows, which I have successfully done.

"Leeza Gibbons gave me great advice a long time ago and said, 'Sometimes you have to accept what you have been given.' I did my very best with this role and am very proud of it. What followed was bigger than anyone could have ever planned."

Beyond honoring the love for the show from its many fans, Haskins also feels that finding your passion and making that passion your focus, rather than more conventional measures of success, is the key to reaching your dreams.

"I guess some people can set out to make money and have that be their goal," he says. "That's just not me. I always make a point at colleges and universities on my speaking tour to ask students to consider how great it would be to make a living doing what you love to do, instead of what you think you are supposed to do. It isn't always going to be easy, but at least you are doing something you love. I love to act and most of what goes with that. I don't want to paint so rosy a picture that it isn't realistic. Sometimes you have to sacrifice a lot to start this part of your journey. But you don't have to give away the farm to do that. You can, and have to, be smart in business too. I believe that doing what you love to do will motivate you a lot more than money. After that, the money will come in whatever form it does, and you can choose how you deal with the money that comes in a result of your hard work."

Doing what you love, as Haskins says, can inspire you to work hard and achieve success. It also puts you in the frame of mind to help others. Your passion, and the fulfillment it brings, creates a positive outlook that will fortify your desire and your efforts to help others achieve their own dreams.

We give that sentiment an A+.

☀ PEOPLE IN CRISIS

Bruce Blythe is CEO of Crisis Management International, a worldwide network of mental health professionals and former FBI agents. He has worked with hundreds of companies dealing with the human side of crisis response and recovery, preparing them for potential crises as well as helping them pick up the pieces after a crisis. In fact, he wrote the book on the subject: *Blindsided: A Manager's Guide to Catastrophic Incidents in the Workplace.*

He has counseled kidnap and ransom hostages after they were freed, has trekked into the jungle of Ecuador, and has assisted families following a school bus crash in Texas in which 23 children were killed. He was there in the aftermath of Hurricane Andrew, as well as at Ground Zero following the attacks on 9/11.

"Ultimately, it's all about people," says Blythe. "My favorite quote of all time is summed up by saying, 'No relationship is any better than its communication.' It's about people's relationships with each other and you and your product, message, or service. I tell people in crisis management in order to make it a simple process and be successful at caring for the people you work with, you must identify people who are impacted and meet their concerns and needs. That's all there is to crisis management.

"Basically two words come to mind that amplify the importance of putting people first. The first is *caring*, and if people don't believe you care about them, then the second word is *outrage*. They become outraged. We must view caring as a behavior or set of behaviors that demonstrate your true values and honest concern about people's well-being. If you come across as a caring, more compliant, more agreeable person or company that stands for values that make the consumer or customer feel valued and respected, they'll like you or your company, be attracted to you, and believe that you are going to be a winner and enhance their life in some way.

"You can't get anything done without people. When you are compassionate, empathetic, and caring, that earns you compassion equity. Even if you mess up or make a mistake, they will still care about you and support you. If you are dedicated to making life better for people, others will support you. It's also the right thing to do. Caring matters. You have to have an inside-out approach and an outside-in approach. Inside-out means [that] I have to have the right ethics [and] character and truly care about the well-being of those customers [and] shareholders, all those things I need to be the right type of person and that needs to exude excellence."

Blythe goes on to state some specific ways to put the care you feel for others into practice by using some of the principles of crisis management:

(1) Deal with people in a caring manner. Put the well-being of people first with caring and compassion.

(2) Assume appropriate responsibility. Take responsibility, and admit when you're wrong.

(3) Address the needs of all individuals in a timely manner. Timing is very important.

(4) Base all decision and actions on legal and ethical guidelines.

(5) Use visible and open communication with all people you deal with.

☀ A PEOPLE'S COURT

Judge Glenda Hatchett became Georgia's first African-American to preside as judge of a state court and department head of one of the largest juvenile court systems in the country. After her first year on the bench, the local chapter of the National Bar Association selected her as "Outstanding Jurist of the Year." On her popular syndicated courtroom reality show that premiered in the fall of 2000, Judge Hatchett offers solutions and real-life lessons to help transform the lives of young people who appear in her court. She also serves as national spokesperson for Court Appointed Special Advocates (CASA), a nonprofit volunteer organization that trains volunteers to represent abused and neglected children and help them to navigate the court system.

"I absolutely believe that God gives us children as an indicator that He believes the world is worthy of continuing and [that] we have to invest there and so deeply in our children and simultaneously in each other," Judge Hatchett says, "because the world must go on, and it must go on in a hopeful and inspiring way. You have to really find your center, whether that's a personal center or corporate center, and be true to it. And all your decisions have to flow from what you believe to be right. If you keep that in front of you, the money will follow.

"No matter who you are, think globally, and think of your piece like a child's Lego piece. You have to figure out how to get your piece of this right and how to interact and network with others and support and encourage each other, and you add your piece to the next person who reaches out to next person. And then you will have a wonderful foundation.

"We all have to ask ourselves, what am I doing that will live beyond our lifetime? What am I prepared to do that I can invest here and now that will live beyond my lifetime? I was told that a Greek philosopher once said, 'We know when civilization has come to a part of the world because men would plant seeds realizing that they would never sit under the shade of the tree.'"

In Judge Hatchett's court, people obviously come first, and people are expected to think beyond themselves and their own needs and concerns, even beyond their own lifetimes. This is how we try to think about success in any business or personal venture: How is my undertaking benefiting others? What mark does it leave on the world? How will it benefit others even after I'm gone. This way of thinking helps to keep the daily ups and downs in perspective. It helps us move from "me" to "we," and with that approach, success has already been achieved.

✳ ROBYN

An amazing story comes to mind that demonstrates this law. The Make-A-Wish Foundation is an amazing organization that is dedicated to granting the wishes of children with life-threatening medical conditions, giving these kids something to look forward to and helping to fulfill their dreams.

The foundation offered to grant a wish to a girl named Hope Stout, a courageous 12-year-old. Hope selflessly wished to help other children in need and asked that all the other children served by the foundation's central and western North Carolina chapter be granted *their* wishes. Hope put the interests of 155 other kids before her own. A syndicated radio show heard about Hope and interviewed her. In four short weeks, donations of over $1.1 million poured in, which enabled the foundation to fulfill Hope's wish for all the other wish kids in her area. At a very young age, Hope Stout died of a rare bone cancer, but she left the world a legacy. True to her name, she understood the importance of the gift of hope and gave it selflessly.

Across the miles, when my daughter Ali, who was then 16 years old, learned about Hope, she was so inspired that she decided to name a handbag she had designed in memory of Hope Stout. After meeting with Hope's family, it was confirmed that the handbag would be called the Handbag of Hope, and a percentage of the proceeds would benefit the foundation to grant wishes. A leading manufacturer agreed to produce the handbag, and a national retailer picked it up and sold it worldwide, contributing almost $500,000 to the foundation to grant wishes.

✳ RICK

No one ever said on his or her tombstone, "I wish I'd spent more time at the office." It seems to me with all the corporate buyouts, it feels like the only thing corporate America cares about is making money. And no amount of money seems to be enough. It's not just the corporations. I see people who work only for money. I don't want to live that way. We all should enjoy going to work. You can find yourself in a job you don't like, and I don't care how much money you're making, at some point you're going to think that this isn't worth it.

People are what make the work important and enjoyable. It's all about the people whom you touch, whom you help, whom you change in some way. We all have an impact on more people than we ever realize. I've been in the book business for a lot of years, and I've met so many wonderful people. And I've also books change lives. A book can change a life, and the author may never know it.

For example, Mike Levine was my mentor and then my partner at Planned Television Arts. He's still one of my best friends, and I still use him as an advisor. In 1982, he begged me to hire his best friend's son, who was just out of college. I taught the kid how to write press releases, and he was here for about six months. Good writer. I lost touch with him, but then I found out that a good friend of his was sick, and he was writing a book to pay for his friend's medical bills. He wasn't writing it to be famous or to get rich. That kid, of course, was Mitch Albom, and the book was *Tuesdays with Morrie*. That book, as we all know, was a huge best-seller.

I've learned that in business and in life if you do things for the right reasons, the universe will pay you back tenfold. Here's an epilogue to that story. Back in 1996, my father was having a hard time. My mother had died six months before, and my father's own health wasn't good, and he was very unhappy. He said, "Rick, do me a favor. Throw me off the balcony." I told him that the bad news is that I can't throw you off the balcony. The good news is that your heart is working at around 5 percent, so you're going to die really soon." Then I handed him a copy of *Tuesdays with Morrie* and said that I thought he'd like it. When he died six years later, I found his wallet among his things, and in his wallet was a piece of paper on which he'd written several quotes from *Tuesdays with Morrie*. Those quotes had kept him going.

That's what I mean about a book being able to change someone's life. That's what we're all trying to do in business—or should be trying to do. Helping each other. Improving each other's lives. It's all about the people you meet along the way and the people you help along the way.

✳ KEEP PEOPLE FIRST

Joe Mark, a veteran hospital executive and the author of *A Cup of Joe, The Prosperity Formula* knows first hand the importance of valuing each other. In the final moments as we concluded the interviews for this book, Joe and his wife were recuperating from a near fatal, very serious accident that happened to them while vacationing. Yet, he still took the time to share this message of concern for others.

"When we keep people first, we set the stage for unlimited levels of prosperity in all of its forms—spiritual, emotional, physical and financial. We have the potential to create loving, customer wowing, highly profitable, and successful businesses. The goal is to make everyone feel genuinely seen, heard, appreciated, respected, and engaged.

"When you put people first, you witness the benefit. From my experiences as a CEO of hospitals and a consultant for 28 years, I was shocked to watch executives walking down hallways and not seeing most of the people they were walking past and not even acknowledging with a hello. People are the bottom line. They are the business. We assume people know how to have great relationships and they don't. That they know how to forgive and the power of reconciliation and sadly, they don't."

Joe adds, "People have to start buzzing about this. I imagine people sitting in mixed groups and talking about what's possible at work if we start treating each other really well. People will be more successful and also feel safe and reinforced. Conversation is the key. This is what I'm passionate about and believe it's about connecting hearts and backing it with good ideas and genuine caring about each other. We have to share ourselves and our knowledge.

"From the boiler room to the boardroom, we can accomplish this together by bringing our passion and the stuff that makes us jump out of bed in the morning to work."

This Joe is clearly a *Wow* in our book!

✳ LAUNCH YOUR WOW!

We hope that you've found information in this book helpful and that it impacts your life in some way. When we started writing, we wanted to provide you with a clear idea of how to make that change and to ignite the spark that will help you to put your ideas into action. Our goal was to help you launch your professional and personal *Wow*—the one you've been waiting or hoping for since you first envisioned your success—the thing you do that catapults first impressions into millions of impressions, the ingredient that separates you from the masses and increases your sales and successes and helps you to build your brand. If you now feel better able to make that launch, writing this book will be a *Wow* success for us.

Remember that, in the end, it's all about how we treat each other and give of ourselves. It's about making other people feel special and appreciated. This is why we're all here—to give without expecting anything in return. When you take this approach, you will be amazed at the invisible gifts you ultimately receive. When you give without asking for anything in return, it doesn't mean you won't get what you deserve. It's simply about doing the right thing. We elevate our own success when we help someone else succeed along the way.

So that's the deal. In a nutshell, the key to *Wow* success. Give to your customers, to your audience, to your allies, to your employees. Come up with an idea that makes everyone's life better, easier, or more fun, and you'll reap the rewards. We believe in the 16 laws, and we believe that if you follow them, you'll make your competition want to be you. And that's a *Wow* thing! Ask yourself every day, "Where's my *Wow*?" and incorporate the *Wow* mentality into your life. Apply the laws, live the laws, and remember that great marketing campaigns work in layers. Follow the advice we've offered and the wisdom of all the experts who generously gave us their time, their insights, and their stories. Make *Wow* a way of life, and make your life a *Wow*! ✳

index

about the authors

Robyn Freedman Spizman is no stranger to success. As an award-winning author and successful entrepreneur, she has written dozens of inspirational and educational nonfiction books during her accomplished career, including *Make It Memorable*, *The GIFTionary*, *When Words Matter Most*, and *The Thank You Book*.

As a veteran media personality and consumer advocate for more than twenty-five years, she has appeared repeatedly on NBC's *Today*, CNN Headline News, and is featured regularly on WXIA-TV (NBC) and WSTR-FM (Star 94) in Atlanta. Her books and advice have been featured extensively in the media including the *New York Times*, *Cosmopolitan*, *Woman's Day*, *Family Circle*, *Redbook*, and *USA Today*.

A nationally sought-after speaker on success, motivational topics, and book writing, Robyn is considered among the most dynamic how-to experts and gift giving authorities in the country. Named one of Atlanta's leading women in business by *Business To Business* magazine, she is regularly featured in media worldwide. Selected as "Ask America's Ultimate Expert" by *Woman's World* magazine, Robyn was also chosen to be amongst an esteemed group of successful business women in North America to participate in the GLOW Project, a documentary where she shares her insights, strategies, and principles about success.

Robyn coauthored many other nonfiction books including *Take This Book To Work* and *The Women For Hire* series with Tory Johnson, CEO and founder of Women For Hire, the *Author 101* book-writing series with Rick Frishman, *Questions To Bring You Closer* series with Stuart Gustafson, and her first two works of fiction for young readers with Mark Johnston titled *Secret Agent* and *The Secret Agents Strike Back*. In addition to her writing, reporting, and speaking, Robyn is the cofounder with her husband, of The Spizman Agency, a highly successful public relations firm that specializes in media relations and book publicity. She also serves on the national advisory council of The Make-A-Wish Foundation and the eWomenNetwork Foundation.

Robyn and her husband Willy live in Atlanta. They have two grown children, Justin (27) and Ali (21) who also are published authors. Visit her Web site at www.robynspizman.com for more information.

Rick Frishman, is the founder of Planned Television Arts, and has been one of the leading book publicists in America for over 30 years. Working with many of the top book editors, literary agents, and publishers in America, including Simon and Schuster, Random House, Wiley, Harper Collins, Pocket Books, Penguin Putnam, and Hyperion Books, he has worked with best-selling authors including Mitch Albom, Bill Moyers, Stephen King, Caroline Kennedy, Howard Stern, President Jimmy Carter, Mark Victor Hansen, Nelson DeMille, John Grisham, Hugh Downs, Henry Kissinger, Jack Canfield, Alan Deshowitz, Arnold Palmer, and Harvey Mackay.

In addition to his work at "PTA," Rick has now taken on the new role as publisher at Morgan James Publishing in New York. David Hancock founded Morgan James in 2003 and in 2007 "MJ" published over 130 books. Morgan James only publishes nonfiction books and looks for authors with a platform who believe in giving back. Morgan James gives a portion of every book sold to Habitat for Humanity. Morgan James Web site is www.morganjamespublishing.com.

Rick has also appeared on hundreds of radio shows and more than a dozen TV shows nationwide, including *OPRAH* and *Bloomberg TV*. He has also been featured in the *New York Times*, *Wall Street Journal*, *Associated Press*, *Selling Power Magazine*, *New York Post* and scores of other publications.

He is the coauthor of eight books, including national best-sellers *Guerrilla Publicity* and *Networking Magic*. Along with media personality Robyn Freedman

Spizman, Rick cowrote the popular four-book series *Author 101*, and recently they teamed up for their highly acclaimed book entitled *Where's Your Wow? 16 Ways To Make Your Competitors Wish They Were You!* (McGraw-Hill, 2008).

He is the cohost (with attorney Richard Solomon) of the radio show *Taking Care of Business*, which airs every Thursday from 2:00–3:00 pm on *WCWP-Radio* in Long Island, New York (www.tcbradio.com). Rick has a B.F.A. in acting and directing and a B.S. from Ithaca College School of Communications and is a sought after lecturer on publishing and public relations, and a member of PRSA and the National Speakers Association.

Rick and his wife Robbi live in Long Island with their three children, Adam, Rachel and Stephanie, and a cockapoo named Rusty. To reach Rick, e-mail him at rick@rickfrishman.com, or go to www.rickfrishman.com for more information and to get Rick's "Million Dollar Rolodex."